CONTENTS

I0178054

SIDE DISHES

DESSERTS

Brain Food

Simple & delicious keto recipes to help prevent Alzheimer's, restore brain health & improve cognitive function

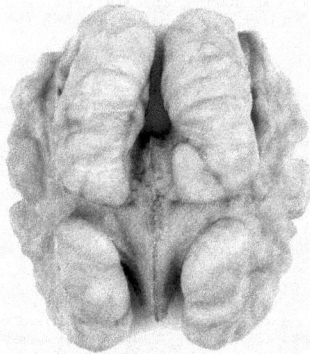

Cooking to Combat Dementia

BRAIN FOOD: COOKING TO COMBAT DEMENTIA
SIMPLE & DELICIOUS KETO RECIPES TO HELP PREVENT ALZHEIMER'S, RESTORE BRAIN HEALTH & IMPROVE COGNITIVE FUNCTION

INTRODUCTION

Take control of your diet and start cooking to combat dementia.

The rise in Alzheimer's disease in Western societies has long been a cause for concern. With better all-round health care keeping us alive longer to enjoy our twilight years, the blight of Alzheimer's is all too real.

Chances are if you're reading this, it's because you or a loved one has started to notice a cognitive decline, or they have an Alzheimer's diagnosis.

Of course, this can be a tremendously difficult time and you are searching for ways - any way at all - to help.

Well, the good news is you don't have to just accept a diagnosis and start planning care and practical requirements.

Studies suggest there is a possibility of reversing some of the side effects of Alzheimer's by changing your diet.

THE CASE FOR KETO
We have known for many years that the brain constantly requires energy and it can either use glucose or ketones as fuel. Usually, the brain uses glucose, which is produced when carbohydrates are broken down. Ketones, on the other hand, are the product of fat being broken down.

It has come to the attention of scientists that changing the fuel the brain uses can have a radical impact. A ketogenic diet has been used as an effective treatment for epilepsy in children since the 1920s. This has prompted research into the possible benefits of a ketogenic diet on other conditions and neurological diseases.

Positive results have been recorded in many patients when eating a ketogenic diet. Improvements have been recorded in mental illnesses, including depression and bipolar disorder as well as brain injury, brain cancer, and migraines.

The premise covering all these illnesses is that the fuel the brain consumes is key to the brain's chemistry and thus, changing the fuel could have a significant effect in terms of treatment.

In addition to a ketogenic diet being looked at as a treatment option for brain illnesses, evidence is coming to light that a typical Western diet could be causing damage to the brain, including the view that the brain is damaged by depriving it of cholesterol, omega 3 fats, and animal fats, and when loading it with oxidised vegetable oils and carbohydrates.

TYPE 3 DIABETES
It's not a stab in the dark to suggest that a ketogenic diet could be an effective treatment for Alzheimer's.

It has been noted that a factor in Alzheimer's is insulin resistance which makes glucose uptake difficult. In fact, this profile of the disease has led many researchers to refer to Alzheimer's as type 3 diabetes.

We know that in Alzheimer's disease, the brain loses its ability to use glucose, but PET (Positron-emission tomography) imaging has shown the brain's use of ketones isn't reduced. This has logically led on to clinical trials to change the brain's fuel source to ketones in Alzheimer's patients.

Several studies have taken place where patients with mild to moderate Alzheimer's ate a ketogenic diet for a period of three months. A significant improvement was recorded in memory tests. However, a month after stopping the diet the improvement had been lost.

There are further clinical trials currently in place to further document and research the ketogenic diet as a treatment path for Alzheimer's and cognitive decline.

Doctors and scientists are concentrating their work on milder and moderate decline. Indeed, people who have resigned and retired due to a cognitive decline have gone back to work after changing to a ketogenic diet.

SO WHAT IS A KETOGENIC DIET?
A ketogenic diet is a very low-carb, high-fat diet. During a keto diet, you significantly reduce carbohydrate intake and replace this with fat. This reduction in carbs puts your body into a metabolic state called ketosis. This means you'll be burning fat for fuel instead of glucose.

This is achieved by eating protein and fat-rich food and avoiding carbohydrates.

Here's a basic overview of the diet:

The foods you'll eat on this diet include:
· Meat: beef, pork, lamb, sausage, bacon, ham, chicken and turkey.
· Fish: fatty fish such as salmon and mackerel, white fish and seafood
· Eggs: fried, poached, scrambled, boiled
· Dairy: full fat milk, butter, and cream. Preferably Grass-fed
· Cheese: unprocessed cheese including hard, soft, cream, sheep, goat, and blue cheese
· Nuts and seeds: Almonds, brazil nuts, pecans, walnuts, flax seeds, hemp seeds, chia seeds, etc.
· Healthy oils and fats: Extra virgin olive oil, coconut oil, avocado oil, ghee, goose fat, and lard
· Low-carb vegetables: Most green vegetables, tomatoes, onions, peppers, etc.
· Some fruits: Including avocados, citrus fruits, some berries, rhubarb, watermelon

Foods you'll avoid on this diet include:
· Sugary foods: cakes, sweets, ice cream, sugary fizzy drinks, table sugar, etc.
· Grains or starches: Rice, pasta, and cereal made from wheat
· Fruit: banana, apples, pears, grapes, tropical fruits
· Beans or legumes: kidney beans, peas, chickpeas and lentils, etc.
· Root vegetables and tubers: carrots, potatoes, parsnips, and sweet potatoes, etc.

If you have a sweet tooth, then you can use a sweetener such as:

- Stevia
- Erythritol
- Monk fruit
- Xylitol
- Allulose
- Yacon Syrup

A NOTE ABOUT FAT

This diet is high in fat and also animal fat. Butter and cream are fine to eat on this diet but an initial hesitance is understandable. It's true that fat has become a four-letter word over the past fifty years. However, there is now a substantial body of researchers who believe heart disease is caused by refined carbohydrates and not saturated fat.

These researchers also point to the fact that heart disease was not an issue before the 1900s until refined carbohydrates became part of a typical diet. Yet that diet was a diet high in dairy and meat products, such as lard and cream.

So, dig in. Fat is delicious!

A NOTE ON NUTRITIONAL KETOSIS:

Achieving ketosis varies from one individual to the next. Typically, you need to reduce your carbs to 5 -10% of your energy intake. This is somewhere usually lower than 50grams of net carbs, and some people need to go lower than 25grams. You can use blood, urine or breath monitors to check if you are in light ketosis. You don't need to be in a high level of ketosis for maximum fat burning. Simply being in ketosis is all that is needed for this Alzheimer's diet.

A WEIGHT LOSS DIET?

Another thing to note is this is not a weight loss diet. The goal here is to achieve mild ketosis; this means the brain will begin to function on ketones. The desired result is an improvement in cognitive function. If anyone following this regime is losing or gaining weight, you should adjust the diet accordingly.

KEEP ON TRACK

In conjunction with the diet, you can inexpensively invest in a ketosis breath analyser. These are far better than keto urine strips and will allow you to monitor ketosis levels. Remember the goal is not optimum ketosis for fat loss; you are just aiming for mild ketosis.

NOT VERY TASTY?

Of course, quality of life is a big factor to consider in all of this. Many people will be concerned that removing the sweet treats and carbohydrates favoured by many negatively impacts quality of life.

Well, first of all, it's not a diet from hell. In fact, this diet gives you the go-ahead to eat many foods, such as butter and cream, which you may have previously abstained from.

Secondly, you may see results remarkably quickly. The great thing about this diet is that it's possible to see results in some people within 48 hours. Most will take longer but it may be noticeable within just two weeks. If you don't see any results within two months, it's still worth persevering a little longer.

An improvement in the cognitive function far outweighs making some dietary changes for many. If you're wondering what you might eat on a Keto diet for cognitive improvement, then take a look at a sample menu below to see what you can eat:

A SAMPLE MENU

For breakfast you might have eggs (fried, scrambled, or poached), with bacon or sausage, and grilled tomatoes. You could also tuck into Keto Pancakes served with whipped cream and blueberries (page 12), or an omelette with a choice of filling such as cheese. You can also add full-fat cream or milk to your morning coffee or tea.

For lunch, have a homemade soup such as Cream of Wild Mushroom (page 26) or Keto French Onion Soup (page 25). You could serve this with a Keto bread roll (page 56), Keto Salad Niçoise (page 24) or a cheese plate with Keto Seed Crackers (page 23).

And for dinner, try delicious Butter Baked Salmon with Lemon and Capers (page 47) served with Broccoli and Cheese Bake (page 68) or melt in the mouth Slow Roasted Beef (page 46).

AND FOR DESSERT?

For dessert, you could have berries served with whipped cream and a square or two of 85% cocoa solid dark chocolate. Or you could have Keto Apple Cobbler (page 90), a Keto Baked Egg Custard Tart (page 92) or a slice of Keto Death by Chocolate Cake (page 91), with whipped cream!

With such delicious recipes and the real possibility of a significant improvement in cognitive function, the ketogenic diet is a very attractive treatment option for many.

Of course, eating keto is a big change. That's why we've put together this comprehensive collection of over 80 easy-to-follow, delicious recipes.

You'll find plenty of carefully devised recipes so you can eat adapted versions of all your favourite meals including main courses, soups, salads, bread, cakes, and desserts.

You should speak to your doctor before making any significant changes to your diet, particularly if you have been prescribed medication or are on an existing food management programme. You must not rely on the information in this book as an alternative to medical advice from your doctor, or other healthcare professional.

Starters, Soups and Snacks

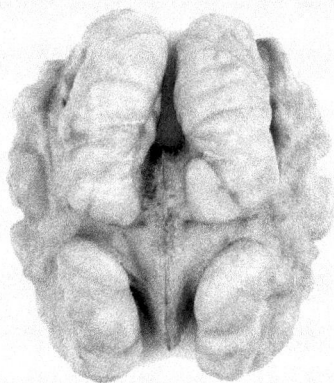

FLUFFY KETO BREAKFAST PANCAKES

NUTRITION (per serving)		
Total Carbs	5	grams
Fibre	3	grams
Net Carbs	2	grams
Protein	13	grams
Fat	39	grams
Calories	425	

Ingredients

For the pancakes:
- 4 eggs
- 200g/7oz cottage cheese
- 1 tbsp psyllium husk powder
- 50g/2oz butter

For the topping:
- 250ml/8½floz double cream, lightly whipped
- 50g/2oz fresh berries such as raspberries, strawberries or blueberries

Method

1 Mix the eggs, cottage cheese, and psyllium husk together in a bowl.

2 Leave the mixture to sit and fluff up for 10 minutes.

3 Melt the butter in a non-stick frying pan.

4 The recipe makes 4 pancakes so using a ladle drop approximately ¼ of the mixture into the hot pan.

5 Maintain a medium-low heat and cook the pancake for 3–4 minutes before flipping. Cook for 3-4 minutes on both sides.

6 Remove the pancakes from the pan and place on a plate.

7 Serve with lightly whipped cream and berries of your choice.

CHEF'S NOTE

These delicious keto pancakes have virtually no net carbs! Serve for a weekend breakfast when you have time to savour them.

SERVES 2

CHEESY KETO CRISPS

NUTRITION (per serving)

Total Carbs	2	grams
Fibre	0	grams
Net Carbs	2	grams
Protein	13	grams
Fat	19	grams
Calories	228	

Ingredients

- 125g/4oz cheddar cheese or edam cheese, grated
- ½ tsp paprika powder

Method

1 Preheat the oven to 400F/200C/ Gas 6.

2 Drop teaspoons of grated cheese in small heaps on a baking sheet lined with greaseproof paper.

3 Ensure you leave space in between each crisp for the cheese to spread out.

4 Top with a little paprika to taste and bake for approximately 8–10 minutes. Keep an eye on the crisps so that the edges don't burn.

5 Remove from the oven and leave to cool before serving.

CHEF'S NOTE
These crisps are delicious served on their own or with a spicy salsa dip.

13

Total Carbs	12	grams
Fibre	8	grams
Net Carbs	4	grams
Protein	5	grams
Fat	41	grams
Calories	417	

SERVES 4

AVOCADO HOUMOUS

Ingredients

- 2 ripe avocados
- 4 tbsp fresh coriander
- 75ml/2½floz olive oil
- 3 tbsp sunflower seeds
- 3 tbsp tahini (sesame paste)
- 1 tbsp lemon juice
- 1 garlic clove, pressed
- ½ tsp ground cumin
- Salt and pepper

Method

1 First prepare the avocado. Cut the avocado in half and take out the stone.

2 Use a spoon to take out the flesh.

3 Including the avocado, pulse all the ingredients in a small food processor or mini blender until smooth.

4 Adjust the oil and lemon juice to adjust the consistency.

5 Adjust the flavouring and seasoning as desired.

CHEF'S NOTE

You can serve the houmous with vegetable crudities or seed crackers. Avocados are a great food to fight Alzheimer's. They are an excellent source of fatty acids, vitamin K and folic acid.

SMOKED SALMON AND AVOCADO

NUTRITION (per serving)

Total Carbs	19	grams
Fibre	13	grams
Net Carbs	6	grams
Protein	58	grams
Fat	71	grams
Calories	911	

Ingredients

- 4 avocados, halved
- 360ml/12½floz crème fraiche or mayonnaise
- 350g/12oz smoked salmon
- 4 tbsp lemon juice
- Salt and pepper

Method

1 Remove the stone from each avocado and place on an individual serving plate.

2 Top each avocado with a spoonful of either mayonnaise or crème fraiche.

3 Now arrange the smoked salmon on top.

4 Season to taste with salt and freshly ground black pepper.

5 Squeeze lemon juice over each avocado to prevent browning.

CHEF'S NOTE

Smoked salmon contains plenty of omega-3 fatty acids linked to a lower risk of Alzheimer's disease. This is a quick, healthy and luxurious starter perfect1 for entertaining.

OVEN-BAKED WALNUT BRIE

NUTRITION (per serving)

Total Carbs	3	grams
Fibre	2	grams
Net Carbs	1	grams
Protein	14	grams
Fat	31	grams
Calories	344	

Ingredients

- 250g/9oz brie cheese or camembert cheese
- 50g/2oz walnuts, finely chopped
- 1 garlic clove, crushed
- 1 tbsp fresh rosemary or fresh thyme
- 1 tbsp olive oil
- Salt and pepper

Method

1 Preheat the oven to 400F/200C/ Gas 6.

2 Place the cheese onto a small non-stick baking tray.

3 Mix the nuts, garlic, herbs and oil together.

4 Place the nut mixture on top of the cheese and season with salt and pepper.

5 Place in the oven and bake for 10 minutes until the cheese is warm and the nuts are toasted.

CHEF'S NOTE
Eating a diet with walnuts has been proven to have positive effects on memory and may reduce the risk of Alzheimer's. Serve with pears, apples, and keto seed crackers for a heavenly dinner party starter.

CREAM OF COURGETTE SOUP

NUTRITION (per serving)

Total Carbs	10	grams
Fibre	3	grams
Net Carbs	7	grams
Protein	4	grams
Fat	1	grams
Calories	60	

Ingredients

- 1 small onion, quartered
- 2 cloves garlic
- 3 medium courgettes, roughly chopped
- 1litre/1½pts chicken or vegetable stock
- 2 tbsp reduced fat crème fraiche
- Salt and pepper to taste

Method

1 Place the onion, garlic, courgette and stock in a large pan and bring to the boil.

2 Leave on a simmering boil for approximately 20 minutes until the courgette is tender.

3 Remove from the heat and process in a food processor until smooth.

4 Return to the pan. Add the crème fraiche and season to taste.

5 Heat through gently to serve.

CHEF'S NOTE
This makes a healthy low-calorie soup. Serve topped with a little Parmesan if desired and seed crackers. Courgettes contain antioxidants thought to promote healthy brain function.

CREAM OF ASPARAGUS SOUP

NUTRITION (per serving)

Total Carbs	7	grams
Fibre	3	grams
Net Carbs	4	grams
Protein	4	grams
Fat	2	grams
Calories	60	

Ingredients

- ½ tbsp unsalted butter
- 1 medium onion, chopped
- 450g/1lb asparagus, stalky ends removed and chopped
- 750ml/1¼pts chicken stock
- 1 tbsp reduced fat crème fraiche
- Salt and pepper, to taste

Method

1 Melt the butter in a large heavy-based pan.

2 Sauté the onion for a few minutes over a low heat.

3 Add the asparagus and pour over the stock.

4 Bring to a boil and simmer for approximately 20 minutes until the asparagus is tender.

5 Use a food processor to blitz the soup until it's smooth.

6 Stir in the crème fraiche.

7 Heat through gently to serve.

CHEF'S NOTE
Asparagus is a brain boosting food high in vitamin K, vitamin C, and folic acid. This soup is great if you're trying to lose weight. Serve with seed crackers or warm keto bread rolls.

KETO POMODORO SAUCE

NUTRITION (per serving)

Total Carbs	4	grams
Fibre	1	grams
Net Carbs	3	grams
Protein	5	grams
Fat	4	grams
Calories	66	

Ingredients

- 2 tbsp extra virgin olive oil
- 4 garlic cloves, crushed
- 2 tsp dried Italian herbs
- 450g/1lb tomato passata
- Erythritol, to taste
- Salt and pepper

Method

1 Sauté the garlic gently in the olive oil in a large heavy based pan for about 3 minutes.

2 Add the tomato passata, herbs, salt and pepper.

3 Bring to the boil and simmer gently covered for around 40 minutes.

4 Add a little sweetener to taste if the sauce is tart.

5 Adjust the seasoning and serve.

6 The sauce can be cooled and stored in the fridge.

CHEF'S NOTE

Tomatoes are thought to protect memory and reduce the risk of Alzheimer's. The sauce is a perfect base for pizza and meat dishes. Or serve simply with roasted squash, olive oil, and parmesan shavings.

KETO CHICKEN STOCK

Ingredients

- 1 chicken
- 1 onion, quartered
- 1 tomato, quartered
- 1 carrot, peeled and roughly chopped
- 2 celery stalks
- 6 cloves garlic
- 2-3 sprigs thyme
- 3 bay leaves
- 8 whole peppercorns
- 1 tsp sea salt

Method

1 Place all the ingredients in a large stock pot.

2 Fill with enough water to cover the chicken completely.

3 Cover and cook for 4 to 8 hours, longer is better.

4 Remove the chicken and reserve for salads and other meals.

5 Remove the bay leaves, peppercorns and vegetables.

6 Cool and then store stock in the fridge in airtight containers. You can skim away any fat that may rise to the top when it has solidified.

CHEF'S NOTE
The collagen in bone stock can assist with depression and neurodegenerative diseases like Alzheimer's. Use as a base for several recipes while the poached chicken can be used for quick meals and snacks.

KALE CRISPS

NUTRITION (per serving)

Total Carbs	5	grams
Fibre	2	grams
Net Carbs	3	grams
Protein	2	grams
Fat	4	grams
Calories	54	

Ingredients

- 100g/3½ oz kale
- ½ tbsp olive oil
- ½ tsp lemon juice
- Sea salt

Method

1 Preheat the oven to 300F/130C/ Gas 2.

2 Wash the kale and pat dry with a tea towel or kitchen paper.

3 Remove any stalky stems.

4 Combine the lemon juice and oil in a large bowl and toss the kale to cover evenly.

5 Line a baking tray with greaseproof paper and arrange the kale in a layer.

6 Bake for 10-15 minutes.

7 Sprinkle with sea salt and enjoy.

CHEF'S NOTE

High in vitamins B6, C, and K, kale is thought to offer protection from Alzheimer's and cognitive decline.

CHICKEN, AVOCADO AND BACON SALAD

NUTRITION (per serving)

Total Carbs	3	grams
Fibre	7	grams
Net Carbs	3	grams
Protein	61	grams
Fat	97	grams
Calories	339	

Ingredients

- 2 eggs
- 75g/3oz bacon, cut into small strips
- 150g/5oz iceberg lettuce
- 1 tomato
- 1 avocado
- ½ cooked chicken, shredded
- 50g/2oz blue cheese, crumbled
- 3 tbsp mayonnaise
- 1 tbsp milk
- Salt and pepper

Method

1 Hard boil the eggs for 8-10 minutes depending on the size and your preference.

2 Shell the eggs and roughly chop them.

3 Fry the bacon pieces over a high heat in a small frying pan until crispy.

4 Roughly chop the lettuce, tomato and avocado and arrange on a large serving plate.

5 Scatter the chicken, bacon, and egg over the salad.

6 Mix the mayonnaise with the milk and salt and pepper.

7 Pour the dressing over the salad and serve straightaway.

CHEF'S NOTE
Eating leafy salad vegetables such as lettuce could be linked to a slower rate of brain ageing and may help stave off dementia and Alzheimer's.

SESAME CRACKERS

NUTRITION (per serving)

Total Carbs	2	grams
Fibre	1	grams
Net Carbs	1	grams
Protein	3	grams
Fat	7	grams
Calories	88	

Ingredients

- 140g/4½oz sesame seeds
- 60g/2½oz sunflower seeds
- 50g/2oz cheese, grated
- 1 tbsp ground psyllium husk powder

- 7 tbsp water
- 2 eggs
- ½ tsp salt

Method

1 Preheat the oven to 350F/180C/ Gas 4.

2 Line a baking tray with greaseproof paper.

3 Mix all the ingredients together and spread out on the baking tray as evenly as possible.

4 Sprinkle sea salt on the crackers and bake for approximately 20 minutes.

5 Remove the crackers and slice into 20 pieces.

6 Turn the oven down to 300F/130C/Gas 2 and return the crackers for 40 minutes.

7 The crackers are done when they are dry all the way through.

8 Store in an airtight container.

CHEF'S NOTE
Sesame seeds are high in zinc, magnesium, and vitamin B6 and are thought to promote memory and brain health. Serve the crackers with cheese or soup.

KETO SALAD NIÇOISE

SERVES 2

NUTRITION (per serving)		
Total Carbs	17	grams
Fibre	6	grams
Net Carbs	11	grams
Protein	34	grams
Fat	85	grams
Calories	957	

Ingredients

For the salad:
- 50g/2oz turnip or celery root, trimmed 7 diced
- 150g/5oz green beans
- 2 tbsp olive oil
- 2 Romaine lettuce
- 60g/2oz tomatoes
- 2 eggs, hardboiled,

- ½ red onion, diced
- 1 160g/5½oz can tuna in olive oil
- 50g/2oz olives

For the dressing:
- ½ tbsp Dijon mustard
- 2 tbsp small capers

- 15g/½oz anchovies
- 75ml/2½floz olive oil
- 4 tbsp mayonnaise
- 1 tbsp fresh parsley
- Juice of ½ lemon
- Salt and pepper

Method

1 Parboil the green beans and the turnip in separate pans for 5 minutes.

2 Leave the turnip to cool.

3 Heat the olive oil in a frying pan and fry the green beans with the garlic.

4 Arrange lettuce leaves on a large serving plate or dish.

5 Top with the green beans, turnip, tomatoes, eggs, onion, tuna and olives.

6 To make the dressing blend all ingredients together thoroughly in a small bowl.

7 Drizzle over the salad and serve immediately.

CHEF'S NOTE
The green beans and lettuce are high in vitamins C, K and folates which provide a boost to the brain. The omega-3 fatty acids found in tuna are known to promote brain health.

FRENCH ONION SOUP

NUTRITION (per serving)

Total Carbs	8	grams
Fibre	1	grams
Net Carbs	7	grams
Protein	24	grams
Fat	46	grams
Calories	543	

Ingredients

- 125g/4oz butter
- 4 medium onions
- 3 garlic cloves
- 1 tsp fresh thyme, finely chopped
- 1litre/1½pts beef bone stock
- ½ tsp xanthan gum
- 225g/8oz gruyere cheese, grated
- 2 bay leaves
- Black pepper

Method

1 Melt the butter in a large heavy based pan or stockpot.

2 Add the onions, garlic and thyme and cook slowly on a low heat until the onions are caramelised for about 30-40 minutes.

3 Pour in the stock and add the bay leaves and xanthan gum. Bring to the boil and simmer for around an hour.

4 To serve, pour the soup into ovenproof bowls, top with cheese and place under a hot grill until the cheese is bubbling and golden.

CHEF'S NOTE
Make beef bone stock in the same way you make chicken stock with bones or a beef joint. The amino acids glycine and arginine may fight inflammation associated with Alzheimer's and other diseases.

CREAM OF WILD MUSHROOM SOUP

SERVES 4

NUTRITION (per serving)

Total Carbs	14	grams
Fibre	3	grams
Net Carbs	11	grams
Protein	6	grams
Fat	45	grams
Calories	468	

Ingredients

- 125g/4oz butter
- 1 shallot, finely chopped
- 150g/5 oz portobello mushrooms, cleaned and roughly chopped
- 150g/5 oz oyster mushrooms, cleaned and roughly chopped
- 150g/5 oz shiitake mushrooms, cleaned and roughly chopped
- 1 garlic clove, crushed
- ½ tsp thyme
- 750ml/1¼pts chicken stock
- 250ml/8½floz double cream
- 225g/8oz celery, roughly chopped

Method

1 Melt the butter in a heavy based pan.

2 Add the vegetables and sauté gently for around 5 to 10 minutes until soft and golden.

3 Add thyme and chicken stock and bring to a boil.

4 Reduce the heat and simmer for around 20 minutes until the celery is tender.

5 Remove from the heat and blend in a food processor in batches with the cream.

6 Heat through gently to serve.

CHEF'S NOTE
Mushrooms contain an antioxidant compound called ergothioneine. It's thought that these and other compounds found in mushrooms may help keep cognitive decline at bay.

CHOCO BREAKFAST SMOOTHIE

NUTRITION (per serving)

Total Carbs	14	grams
Fibre	12	grams
Net Carbs	2	grams
Protein	5	grams
Fat	35	grams
Calories	350	

Ingredients

- 1 medium avocado
- 250ml/8½floz coconut milk
- 4 tbsp cocoa powder
- 1 tsp vanilla extract
- 2 tbsp chia seeds
- Pinch of sea salt
- Erythritol, to taste
- Ice
- Water

Method

1 Cut the avocado in half, take out the stone and scoop the flesh into a blender.

2 Now add the coconut milk, cocoa powder, vanilla extract, chia seeds, salt, an erythritol and blend until smooth.

3 Add water or ice and blend to desired consistency.

4 Pour into 2 glasses and enjoy.

CHEF'S NOTE

This creamy smoothie packs a boost for the brain with flavonoids in cocoa and folates in avocado. It also packs a big fibre boost from the chia seeds.

COURGETTE CRUSTED PIZZA

NUTRITION (per serving)

Total Carbs	15	grams
Fibre	2	grams
Net Carbs	13	grams
Protein	21	grams
Fat	18	grams
Calories	330	

Ingredients

For the base:
- 2 large eggs, lightly beaten
- 300g/11oz courgette, grated and squeezed dry
- 50g/2oz mozzarella, grated
- 50g/2oz parmesan, grated
- 25g/1oz plain flour
- 1 tbsp olive oil
- 1 tbsp fresh basil, finely chopped
- 1 tsp fresh thyme, finely chopped

For the topping:
- 350g/12oz roasted sweet red peppers, cut into strips
- 100g/3½oz mozzarella cheese
- 75g/3oz pepperoni, sliced thinly

Method

1 Preheat oven to 450F/230C/ Gas 8.

2 Combine all the ingredients for the base in a large bowl.

3 Spread the mixture out onto a 30cm/12-inch pizza pan.

4 Bake until a light golden colour, about 12-15 minutes.

5 Add the toppings and return to the oven for another 10 minutes or until the cheese is bubbling.

6 Serve straightaway with a green salad.

CHEF'S NOTE
Several components of courgette, including potassium and folate, are known to provide neurological benefits. Folate reduces the occurrence of Alzheimer's and potassium has been linked to increased blood flow to the brain.

SWEET PEPPER FRITTATA

NUTRITION (per serving)

Total Carbs	10	grams
Fibre	8	grams
Net Carbs	2	grams
Protein	18	grams
Fat	16	grams
Calories	260	

Ingredients

- 8 large eggs
- 125g/4oz cup ricotta cheese
- 2 tbsp lemon juice
- ½ tsp salt
- ¼ tsp pepper
- 1 tbsp olive oil

- 225g/8oz fresh asparagus spears, woody stems removed and cut into pieces
- 175g/6oz onion, thinly sliced
- 75g/3oz red and green pepper, thinly sliced
- 25g/1oz portobello mushrooms, thinly sliced

Method

1 Preheat oven to 350F/180C/Gas 4.

2 Whisk the eggs, ricotta, lemon juice and salt and pepper together in a large bowl.

3 Heat the oil in a frying pan.

4 Sauté the asparagus, onion, peppers and mushrooms until soft.

5 Place the vegetables in an ovenproof 25cm/10-inch tin.

6 Pour over the egg mixture and bake for 20-25 minutes or until eggs are completely set.

7 Cut into 8 wedges and serve 2 wedges per person with a light green salad for a delicious light lunch.

CHEF'S NOTE
Asparagus is packed with vitamins A, K, B, folate and chromium. All of these help protect the brain against moderate cognitive decline and Alzheimer's.

COCONUT CURRY CAULIFLOWER SOUP

NUTRITION (per serving)		
Total Carbs	12	grams
Fibre	8	grams
Net Carbs	4	grams
Protein	4	grams
Fat	10	grams
Calories	139	

Ingredients

- 1 tbsp olive oil
- 1 medium onion, finely chopped
- 2 tbsp yellow curry paste
- 450g/1lb cauliflower, broken into florets
- 450ml/15½floz vegetable or chicken stock
- 120ml/4floz coconut milk
- Fresh coriander, finely chopped

Method

1 Heat the oil in a stock pot over a medium heat.

2 Fry the onion until soft.

3 Add the curry paste and cook for a further 2 minutes.

4 Add the cauliflower and the stock and bring to the boil.

5 Simmer for around 20 minutes or until the cauliflower is tender.

6 Puree the soup in batches in a food processor.

7 Stir in the coconut milk and heat through gently to serve.

8 Top with coriander to serve.

CHEF'S NOTE
It's believed curcumin in curry spice helps to break down clumps of beta-amyloid protein linked to Alzheimer's. India, where curry spice is a staple, has one of the world's lowest rates of Alzheimer's.

KETO BREAKFAST MUFFINS

NUTRITION (per serving)

Total Carbs	16	grams
Fibre	5	grams
Net Carbs	11	grams
Protein	7	grams
Fat	14	grams
Calories	213	

Ingredients

- 125g/4oz golden flaxseed meal
- 25g/1oz cocoa powder
- 1 tbsp cinnamon
- ½ tbsp baking powder
- ½ tsp salt
- 1 large egg
- 2 tbsp coconut oil, melted
- 60ml/2floz syrup sweetener
- 150g/5oz ripe bananas, mashed
- 1 tbsp lemon juice
- 1 tbsp milk
- 1 tsp vanilla extract
- 1 tsp apple cider vinegar
- 25g/1oz slivered almonds

Method

1 Preheat the oven to 350F/180C/ Gas 4.

2 Line a muffin tin with 6 large muffin cases.

3 Mix all the ingredients together well in a large bowl.

4 Drop the mixture into the muffin cases.

5 Top with the almonds.

6 Bake for approximately 15 minutes until risen and set.

CHEF'S NOTE

It's thought that foods rich in omega-3 fatty acids may help protect against Alzheimer's disease. Flax seeds have the highest amount of omega-3 fatty acids content of any known food.

KETO PORRIDGE

NUTRITION (per serving)

Total Carbs	20	grams
Fibre	14	grams
Net Carbs	6	grams
Protein	18	grams
Fat	13	grams
Calories	249	

Ingredients

- 2 tbsp coconut flour
- 3 tbsp golden flaxseed meal
- 2 tbsp vanilla protein powder
- 360ml/12½floz unsweetened almond milk
- Powdered erythritol to taste

Method

1 Mix the coconut flour, flaxseed meal, and protein powder together in a heavy based sauce pan.

2 Pour in the milk and stir well.

3 Cook over a low-medium heat until thickened.

4 Add sweetener to taste.

5 Serve with a berry topping if desired.

CHEF'S NOTE

Swapping cow's milk for almond milk makes this breakfast rich in vitamin E. Flax seed meal gives an omega-3 boost.

Main Dishes

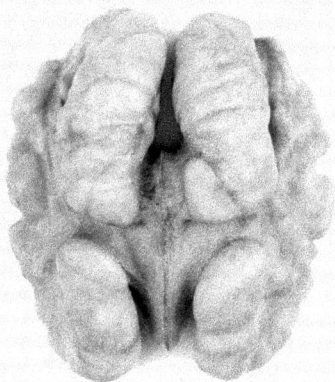

CHICKEN ROULADE WITH DIJON SAUCE

NUTRITION (per serving)

Total Carbs	5.5	grams
Fibre	1.2	grams
Net Carbs	1.4	grams
Protein	43.9	grams
Fat	35.9	grams
Calories	544	

Ingredients

For the chicken:
- 4 chicken breasts
- 8 slices of prosciutto
- 140g/4½oz gruyere cheese, grated
- 50g/2oz sundried tomatoes, chopped
- 4 large eggs, beaten
- 100g/3½oz flax meal
- 50g/2oz parmesan cheese, grated
- 2 tsp garlic salt
- ½ tsp pepper
- 4 tbsp extra virgin olive oil

For the Dijon sauce:
- 50g/2oz butter
- 3 tbsp Dijon mustard
- 150ml/5floz double cream
- Salt and pepper, to taste

Method

1 Preheat oven to 350F/175C/Gas 4.

2 Butterfly the chicken breasts and place between clingfilm.

3 Use a meat mallet to flatten the chicken until they are about ½ cm thick.

4 Top the chicken breast with 2 slices of prosciutto, cheese, and tomatoes.

5 Roll the chicken breast up into a sausage-shaped parcel by using the clingfilm and twisting the ends of the clingfilm closed.

6 Mix the flax meal, parmesan, garlic salt, thyme, and pepper on a plate.

7 Now unwrap the chicken and dip in the beaten egg and then in the flax meal mix.

8 Place the chicken breasts on a baking sheet, drizzle with the olive oil and bake for 25 minutes.

9 To make the sauce simply place all the ingredients in a small non-stick saucepan. Bring to a simmer and cook gently until it has reduced slightly.

10 To serve, slice the chicken roulade and drizzle the sauce around.

KETO QUICHE LORRAINE

NUTRITION (per serving)		
Total Carbs	7	grams
Fibre	2	grams
Net Carbs	5	grams
Protein	26	grams
Fat	85	grams
Calories	897	

Ingredients

For the pie crust:
- 125g/4oz almond flour
- 40g/1½oz sesame seeds
- 1 tbsp ground psyllium husk powder
- ½ tsp salt
- 1 egg
- 50g/2oz butter

For the custard:
- Knob of butter

- 300g/11oz smoked bacon
- 1 onion, finely chopped
- 250ml/8½floz double cream
- 225g/8oz cheddar cheese, grated
- 5 eggs
- ½ tsp salt
- ¼ tsp pepper

Method

1 Preheat oven to 350F/175C/Gas 4.

2 Place all the pie crust ingredients in a food processor and pulse until it forms a stiff dough.

3 Use a spatula to spread the dough into a 20cm/8-inch springform tin. You can use a sheet of greaseproof paper under the pie crust for easier removal later. Chill in the fridge.

4 Fry the bacon and onion in the butter gently until the onion is soft and translucent.

5 Whisk the cream, eggs, and cheese together to make the savoury custard.

6 Add the bacon and onion to the pie crust and pour in the custard

7 Bake in the oven for around 45 minutes until the quiche is puffed up and golden.

8 Delicious served warm with a salad.

CHEF'S NOTE
The psyllium husk helps to make the dough more elastic and workable. It's also a great source of fibre and can reduce blood sugar.

KETO BEEF STROGANOFF

NUTRITION (per serving)

Total Carbs	9	grams
Fibre	3	grams
Net Carbs	6	grams
Protein	27	grams
Fat	31	grams
Calories	420	

Ingredients

For the stroganoff:
- 50g/2oz butter
- 140g/4½oz mushrooms, sliced
- Salt and pepper
- 450g/1lb sirloin or fillet steak, sliced into thin strips
- 1 red onion, chopped
- 1 tbsp tomato puree
- 100ml/3½floz beef stock
- 100ml/3½floz crème fraiche

For the cabbage noodles:
- 25g/1oz butter
- ½ large head of green cabbage, thinly sliced
- 1 tbsp water
- Salt and pepper

Method

1 Heat half of the butter in a frying pan and fry the mushrooms for 5 minutes until softened. Set aside in a bowl.

2 Add the beef to the pan and brown for 5 minutes. Set aside with the mushrooms.

3 Melt the remaining butter and sauté the onions until translucent.

4 Whisk in the tomato puree, gradually add the stock.

5 Now return the beef and mushrooms to the pan.

6 Reduce the heat and stir in the crème fraiche.

7 For the noodles, melt the butter in a large heavy based saucepan.

8 Add the cabbage, water, and seasoning and cook on low heat until tender.

9 Place the noodles on a plate and top with the stroganoff.

CHEF'S NOTE
It's worth paying extra and buying fillet for this dish - because you are only serving around 100g/4oz of beef per person it won't break the bank.

CHILLI SALMON WITH SPINACH

NUTRITION (per serving)

Total Carbs	5	grams
Fibre	3	grams
Net Carbs	2	grams
Protein	43	grams
Fat	59	grams
Calories	717	

Ingredients

- 350g/12oz salmon, in 2 pieces
- ½ tbsp chilli paste
- 120ml/4floz crème fraiche or mayonnaise
- 2 tbsp parmesan cheese, grated
- 225g/8oz fresh spinach
- 25g/1oz butter
- Salt and pepper

Method

1 Preheat the oven to 400F/200C/ Gas 6.

2 Grease a baking dish with half of the butter.

3 Place the seasoned salmon in the greased baking dish.

4 Mix together the crème fraiche, chilli paste and parmesan cheese.

5 Spread the mixture over the salmon and bake for 15–20 minutes

6 While the salmon is cooking, wilt the spinach in the remaining butter.

7 Season the spinach and serve immediately with the salmon.

CHEF'S NOTE

A perfect weekday evening meal ready in minutes. Eating omega 3-rich salmon and spinach high in folic acid can help prevent Alzheimer's.

CHEESE AND HAM CRUSTLESS QUICHE

NUTRITION (per serving)

Total Carbs	5	grams
Fibre	2	grams
Net Carbs	3	grams
Protein	30	grams
Fat	19	grams
Calories	325	

Ingredients

- 1 tsp olive oil
- 175g/6oz broccoli, chopped and steamed
- 250g/9oz ham, roughly diced
- 4 tbsp single cream
- 175ml/6floz semi-skimmed milk
- 5 large eggs
- 125g/4oz cheddar cheese, grated
- Salt and pepper

Method

1 Preheat oven to 350F/180C/ gas 4.

2 Use a pastry brush to brush the base and sides of a flan dish with oil.

3 Scatter the broccoli and the ham into the flan dish.

4 Mix the cream, milk, eggs and cheese together in a jug.

5 Pour the custard into the dish.

6 Bake in the oven for around 35 minutes or until golden and set.

7 Cut the quiche into 4 pieces and serve.

CHEF'S NOTE
Broccoli is a great source of folic acid, which is thought to reduce the risk of Alzheimer's.

KETO CHICKEN CACCIATORE

NUTRITION (per serving)

Total Carbs	28	grams
Fibre	2	grams
Net Carbs	26	grams
Protein	14	grams
Fat	6	grams
Calories	252	

Ingredients

- 8 skinless chicken thighs
- 1 tbsp olive oil
- ½ red pepper, sliced
- ½ green pepper, sliced
- 1 medium onion, sliced
- 800g/1¾lb chopped tomatoes
- 1 tsp Italian herbs
- 1 bay leaf
- Salt and pepper

Method

1 Season the chicken with salt and black pepper.

2 Brown the chicken and gently fry the vegetables in a large heavy-based pan.

3 Pour over the tomatoes.

4 Add the bay leaves, herbs and salt and pepper.

5 Cover the pan and cook for 1 to 1½ hours.

6 Remove the bay leaves. adjust the seasoning and serve.

CHEF'S NOTE

Enjoy this low-calorie dish with roasted squash and steamed broccoli.

SERVES 4

KETO PULLED PORK RAGU

NUTRITION (per serving)

Total Carbs	16	grams
Fibre	0	grams
Net Carbs	16	grams
Protein	4	grams
Fat	3	grams
Calories	232	

Ingredients

- 550g/1lb4oz pork tenderloin
- 1 tsp sea salt
- Black pepper
- 1 tbsp olive oil
- 5 cloves garlic, crushed
- 800g/1¾lb chopped tomatoes
- 100g/7oz roasted red peppers
- 3 sprigs fresh thyme
- 5 bay leaves

Method

1 Season pork with salt and pepper.

2 Brown the pork and garlic in a large heavy-based pan for 2 to 3 minutes.

3 Add the remaining ingredients and bring to the boil.

4 Reduce to a simmer and cover the pan.

5 Cook for 2 hours until the pork shreds easily.

6 Remove the bay leaves, shred with a fork and serve.

CHEF'S NOTE
Serve with fresh chopped parsley and courgettucine.

ZAATAR LAMB CHOPS

NUTRITION (per serving)		
Total Carbs	1	grams
Fibre	0	grams
Net Carbs	1	grams
Protein	33	grams
Fat	8	grams
Calories	206	

Ingredients

- 1 tbsp olive oil
- 3 cloves garlic, crushed
- 8 lamb loin chops, trimmed
- ½ fresh lemon
- 1 tsp sea salt
- 1 tbsp Zaatar seasoning

Method

1 Place the oil and garlic in a bowl and rub over the lamb chops.

2 Place the chops on a grill pan and squeeze the lemon over both sides of the chops.

3 Season both sides of the chops with the salt, pepper and Zaatar spice.

4 Grill under a preheated grill on medium heat for 3 to 5 minutes each side.

5 Set aside chops when cooked as desired according to taste. 3 minutes will give you a pink chop and in 5 minutes it should be well done.

6 Serve with accompaniments.

CHEF'S NOTE

If you haven't used Zaatar before, it's a Middle eastern spice blend with thyme and sesame. Serve with cauliflower rice and wilted spinach.

GARLIC AND LIME PORK CHOPS

NUTRITION (per serving)

Total Carbs	1	grams
Fibre	0	grams
Net Carbs	1	grams
Protein	30	grams
Fat	6	grams
Calories	224	

Ingredients

- 2 lean boneless pork chops
- ½ lime, juiced
- 1 tsp lime zest
- 2 cloves garlic, crushed
- ½ tsp cumin
- ½ tsp chilli powder
- ½ tsp paprika
- Salt and pepper

Method

1 Trim any fat from the pork.

2 Put the lime, garlic, cumin, chilli powder, paprika, salt and pepper in a large bowl.

3 Rub the pork chops in the marinade and leave for 2 hours or overnight.

4 Place the chops on a grill pan and cook for about 5 minutes each side under a medium high heat.

5 Season with salt and pepper and serve garnished with lime wedges.

CHEF'S NOTE

Paprika, chilli and cumin are thought to protect against Alzheimer's. The chops are delicious served with Courgettucine and Keto Onion Rings.

PAN-FRIED FISH WITH CAPERS

NUTRITION (per serving)

Total Carbs	7	grams
Fibre	1	grams
Net Carbs	6	grams
Protein	2	grams
Fat	43	grams
Calories	271	

Ingredients

- 2 tsp butter
- 2 cloves garlic, crushed
- ½ lemon, juiced
- 60ml/2floz white wine
- 2 175g/6oz fish fillets, skinned and boned
- 2 tsp capers
- 120ml/4floz pomodoro sauce
- Salt and pepper

Method

1 Melt butter in a large frying pan over medium heat.

2 Sauté the garlic for 2 minutes until fragrant.

3 Add the lemon juice and wine and reduce for 1 minute.

4 Now add the fish fillets, capers, and pomodoro sauce.

5 Cover and cook for 4 minutes and then turn the fillets over.

6 Cook for another 2 minutes or until completely cooked through.

7 Adjust the seasoning and serve immediately.

CHEF'S NOTE

This is a super healthy and delicious dish. Halibut, plaice, hake and all kinds of fish work well with this dish. Serve with courgettucine or wilted spinach.

ABERDEEN ANGUS KEBABS

NUTRITION (per serving)

Total Carbs	5	grams
Fibre	1	grams
Net Carbs	4	grams
Protein	20	grams
Fat	13	grams
Calories	219	

Ingredients

- 400g/14oz Angus beef, cut into 2cm cubes
- Sea salt and fresh ground pepper
- 1 medium red onion, cut into large chunks
- 12 cherry tomatoes

For the Chimichurri Sauce:
- 2 tbsp parsley, finely chopped
- 2 tbsp coriander, finely chopped
- 2 tbsp red onion, finely chopped
- 2 cloves garlic, crushed
- 2 tbsp extra virgin olive oil
- 2 tbsp apple cider vinegar
- 1 tbsp water
- ¼ tsp crushed chilli flakes
- Salt and pepper

Method

1 Before you begin cooking soak 4 bamboo skewers in water for an hour.

2 Make the chimichurri sauce in advance by combining all ingredients in a jar and shaking. Store in the fridge for later.

3 Season the beef with salt and pepper.

4 Thread the beef, onions, and tomatoes onto the skewers and place on a grill rack.

5 Preheat the grill to high and cook for 2-4 minutes per side depending on if you prefer rare or well-done steak.

6 Transfer to serving plates and drizzle with the chimichurri sauce.

CHEF'S NOTE
Coriander is packed with vitamin K which is thought to stimulate memory and helps delay the onset of memory conditions like Alzheimer's.

SAUSAGES AND CREAMY CABBAGE

NUTRITION (per serving)		
Total Carbs	17	grams
Fibre	5	grams
Net Carbs	12	grams
Protein	47	grams
Fat	112	grams
Calories	1260	

Ingredients

- 350g/12oz high-quality sausage
- 15g/½oz butter
- 175g/6oz green cabbage, sliced thinly
- 15g/½oz butter
- 75ml/2½floz double cream
- Salt and pepper
- 2 tbsp fresh parsley, finely chopped

Method

1 Fry the sausage in butter in a frying pan while you prepare the cabbage.

2 Sauté the cabbage in the remaining butter for a few minutes in large frying pan until it begins to brown.

3 Add the cream and gently boil.

4 Reduce the cream by half then season with salt and pepper.

5 Serve the cabbage on hot serving plates with the sausage.

CHEF'S NOTE

Green cabbage is rich in both vitamin K and vitamin C. Both of these have anti-inflammatory and antioxidant properties thought to improve memory and reduce Alzheimer's risk.

SLOW ROASTED BEEF

NUTRITION (per serving)

Total Carbs	9	grams
Fibre	2	grams
Net Carbs	7	grams
Protein	56	grams
Fat	10	grams
Calories	378	

Ingredients

- 900g-1.375kg/2-3lb beef roast, such as a boneless shoulder roast
- Sea salt or celery salt
- Freshly ground black pepper
- 2 carrots, peeled and roughly chopped
  2 ribs celery, trimmed and roughly chopped
- 1 onion, quartered
- 1 head garlic, sliced through to expose the cloves

For the sauce:
- 120ml/4floz dry red wine
- 120ml/4floz homemade beef bone broth

Method

1 Preheat the oven to 400F/200C/Gas 6.

2 Season the beef with salt and pepper and sear on all sides in a large frying pan.

3 Place the vegetables in a single layer on the bottom of a roasting pan and place the beef on top with the fat layer uppermost.

4 Place in the oven and immediately reduce the temperature to 325F/170/Gas 3.

5 Cook for 2 ½ hours per pound for medium-rare.

6 Allow to rest for 15-20 minutes

before carving the beef.

7 To make the sauce squeeze the cloves from the cooked head of the garlic into a small blender.

8 Add the remaining vegetables from the pan and pulse until finely chopped.

9 Put the vegetables, wine and broth into a small saucepan and cook for 30 minutes.

10 Strain through a sieve, return to the pan, season to taste and reduce a little more to intensify the flavour if desired.

11 Serve with the beef.

BUTTER BAKED SALMON

NUTRITION (per serving)

Total Carbs	3	grams
Fibre	1	grams
Net Carbs	2	grams
Protein	28	grams
Fat	26	grams
Calories	323	

Ingredients

- 2 150g/5oz salmon fillets
- Salt and pepper
- 60g/2oz butter
- 4 lemon slices

- 2 tbsp capers
- 1 tsp lemon zest
- Juice of ½ lemon
- Sea salt and fresh cracked pepper

Method

1 Preheat oven to 400F/200C/ Gas 6.

2 Line a baking sheet with aluminium foil and brush with oil.

3 Arrange the salmon on the baking tray on top of the foil.

4 Season with salt and pepper, dot with one third of the butter and top with lemon slices.

5 Bake for 10 minutes.

6 Remove from the oven and use the foil to create a sealed parcel for the fish for 10 further minutes.

7 To make the sauce melt the butter with capers, juice, zest and salt and pepper.

8 Cook for 2 minutes.

9 To serve pour the lemon caper butter over the fish.

CHEF'S NOTE

Salmon is high in DHA and omega-3 fatty acids, and research has proven that DHA reduces the risk of dementia. Serve with broccoli for a delicious brain boosting light meal.

MEXICAN STUFFED PEPPERS

NUTRITION (per serving)

Total Carbs	9	grams
Fibre	3	grams
Net Carbs	6	grams
Protein	33	grams
Fat	24	grams
Calories	375	

Ingredients

- 350g/12oz cauliflower rice
- 500g/1lb2oz minced turkey
- 125g/4oz Monterey jack cheese or gouda, grated
- 1 tsp garlic powder
- 1 tsp chilli powder
- 1 tsp onion powder
- ½ tsp crushed red pepper flakes
- ¼ tsp dried oregano
- ½ tsp paprika
- ¼ tsp cumin
- ¼ tsp cayenne pepper
- 1 ½ tbsp olive oil
- 4 large red peppers, halved and deseeded

Method

1 Preheat oven to 350F/180C/ Gas 4.

2 Put all the spices in a large bowl.

3 Add the minced turkey and mix until the spices are combined.

4 Heat the oil in a heavy-based and fry the mince, breaking into pieces as it cooks.

5 Cook the mince for 6-8 minutes then leave to cool.

6 Stir in the cauliflower and olive oil.

7 Place the pepper halves into a baking dish and spoon the filling into the shells.

8 Top with the cheese then bake in the oven for 25-30 minutes.

9 Serve with a green salad.

CHEF'S NOTE
Results suggest that red pepper consumption might be an effective intervention for preventing age-related memory deficit.

AUBERGINE PARMIGIANA

NUTRITION (per serving)

Total Carbs	12	grams
Fibre	8	grams
Net Carbs	4	grams
Protein	19	grams
Fat	28	grams
Calories	375	

Ingredients

- 1 large aubergine, sliced into 8 approximate 1cm slices
- Sea salt
- 75g/3oz parmesan cheese, grated
- 40g/1½oz flaxseed meal
- ½ tbsp Italian herbs
- 1 large egg
- 4 tbsp butter, melted
- 250ml/8½floz pomodoro tomato sauce
- 125g/4oz mozzarella, grated

Method

1 Preheat the oven to 400F/200C/ Gas 6.

2 Place the aubergine slices on a tea towel and sprinkle with sea salt. Set aside for 30 minutes.

3 Mix the parmesan, flaxseed meal, Italian seasoning together in a shallow bowl.

4 Beat the egg in a separate shallow dish.

5 Melt the butter and pour into a baking dish 20cm by 30cm.

6 Pat each aubergine slice dry. Dip in the beaten egg, them the parmesan mixture and place in the dish.

7 Bake the aubergine for 20 minutes then turn and bake for another 20 minutes.

8 Top with the pomodoro sauce and the mozzarella.

9 Return to the oven for a further 5-10 minutes until the cheese is bubbling and golden.

10 Serve 2 slices per person.

CHEF'S NOTE

Anthocyanin nasunin has been associated with inhibiting brain and central nervous system neural degeneration, so aubergine may be another food that helps prevent Alzheimer's.

CREAMY PORK MEDALLIONS

NUTRITION (per serving)

Total Carbs	1	grams
Fibre	0	grams
Net Carbs	1	grams
Protein	25	grams
Fat	23	grams
Calories	317	

Ingredients

- 450g/1lb pork tenderloin, sliced into 12 pieces
- 2 cloves of garlic, crushed
- 1 tsp dried dill
- 1 tsp dried coriander
- ½ tsp red pepper flakes
- Salt and pepper
- 25g/1oz butter
- 50g/2oz blue cheese, crumbled
- 120ml/4floz double cream
- 1 tbsp fresh parsley, finely chopped

Method

1 Sprinkle the pork with the garlic, dill, coriander, red pepper flakes and salt and pepper.

2 Melt the butter in a large frying pan and sauté the pork for 3-5 minutes each side, or until cooked through.

3 Add the cream and bring to the boil.

4 When the cream has thickened slightly, stir in the cheese.

5 Sprinkle with parsley to serve.

CHEF'S NOTE
Serve the medallions with oven-baked turnip wedges and courgettucinne.

COD AND
ASPARAGUS BAKE

NUTRITION (per serving)

Total Carbs	6	grams
Fibre	2	grams
Net Carbs	4	grams
Protein	23	grams
Fat	3	grams
Calories	141	

Ingredients

- 4 cod fillets (125g/4oz each)
- 450g/1lb fresh thin asparagus, trimmed
- 2 tbsp lemon juice
- 1 tsp grated lemon zest
- 300g/11oz cherry tomatoes, halved
- 40g/1½oz Romano or parmesan cheese, grated

Method

1 Preheat oven to 375F/190C/ Gas 5.

2 Brush a 30cm by 20cm baking tray with oil.

3 Arrange the cod and asparagus in the tray.

4 Squeeze the lemon juice over the fish and top with lemon zest.

5 Put the cherry tomatoes in the baking tray with the cut side facing down.

6 Finally sprinkle with the cheese and bake for around 15 minutes.

7 Serve immediately.

CHEF'S NOTE

It's not just oily fish that's good for your brain. Cod is a good source of phosphorus, niacin, and Vitamin B-12. Deficiencies in niacin and vitamin B-12 have been linked to Alzheimer's.

CREAMY DILL CHICKEN

NUTRITION (per serving)

Total Carbs	8	grams
Fibre	2	grams
Net Carbs	6	grams
Protein	39	grams
Fat	9	grams
Calories	274	

Ingredients

- 4 chicken breasts (175g/6oz each)
- ½ tsp garlic salt
- ¼ tsp pepper
- 1 tbsp olive oil
- 600g/1lb5oz fresh broccoli florets
- 250ml/8½floz fresh chicken stock
- 1 tbsp plain flour
- 250ml/8½floz semi-skimmed milk
- 1 tbsp fresh dill, finely chopped

Method

1 Season the chicken with salt and pepper.

2 Heat the oil in a large frying pan and brown the chicken thoroughly on both sides. Set aside.

3 Add the broccoli and the stock to the frying pan and bring to the boil.

4 Reduce the heat and simmer to cook the broccoli until tender, about 3-5 minutes.

5 Remove the broccoli and keep warm.

6 In a small bowl blend the flour into the milk.

7 Add the milk and dill to the pan and cook for 2 minutes until the sauce has thickened.

8 Return the chicken to the pan and cook for a further 10 minutes until the chicken is completely cooked.

9 Serve with the broccoli.

CHEF'S NOTE

Sulforaphane, which is found in broccoli, protects the brain. Broccoli is also high in Alzheimer's-fighting vitamin C, vitamin K, iron and potassium.

RED COCONUT CURRY

NUTRITION (per serving)

Total Carbs	8	grams
Fibre	4	grams
Net Carbs	4	grams
Protein	4	grams
Fat	41	grams
Calories	398	

Ingredients

- 4 tbsp coconut oil
- ½ medium onion, finely chopped
- 1 tsp garlic, crushed
- 200g/7oz broccoli florets
- 250g/9oz spinach
- 1 tsp ginger, crushed
- 2 tsp fish sauce
- 2 tsp soy sauce
- 1 tbsp red curry paste
- 120ml/4floz coconut cream

Method

1 Melt the coconut oil in a large wok.

2 Fry the onion and garlic until soft.

3 Add the broccoli to the pan and cook for 2-3 minutes. Push broccoli to one side of the wok.

4 Now add the curry paste and let cook for 1 minute in the middle of the wok.

5 Add the spinach and allow to wilt slightly.

6 Add the coconut cream, soy sauce, fish sauce, and ginger.

7 Let simmer for 5-10 minutes.

8 Serve with cauliflower rice.

CHEF'S NOTE
Consider having a daily serving of a leafy green like spinach. The vitamin K is thought to slow cognitive decline.

CARROT AND COURGETTE PIE

NUTRITION (per serving)

Total Carbs	27	grams
Fibre	17	grams
Net Carbs	10	grams
Protein	29	grams
Fat	110	grams
Calories	1170	

Ingredients

For the pastry:
- 100g/3½oz sunflower seeds
- 1 tbsp sesame seeds
- 100g/3½oz coconut flour
- 4 eggs
- 150g/5 oz butter, melted
- 1 tbsp ground psyllium husk powder
- 1 tsp salt

For the filling:
- 150g/5oz courgette, sliced thinly lengthwise
- 75g/3oz carrots, peeled and thinly sliced lengthwise
- 8 eggs
- 300ml/10½floz mayonnaise
- 1 tsp onion powder
- Salt and pepper

Method

1 Blitz the seeds in a food processor until you have a coarse flour.

2 Add the remaining ingredients and pulse to form a dough.

3 Chill the dough in the fridge for 30 minutes.

4 Roll the dough between two pieces of clingfilm and use to fill a 22cm/9-inch flan tin.

5 Bake in a preheated oven of 400F/200C/Gas 6 for 5-7 minutes. Leave to cool.

6 Arrange the strips of carrot and courgette in rolled bundles that resemble flowers inside the crust base.

7 Blend the eggs, mayonnaise, onion powder and salt and pepper.

8 Pour the egg mixture carefully into the dish.

9 Bake for 20-25 minutes at 350F/180C/Gas 4 until set.

10 Serve with a green salad.

Side
Dishes

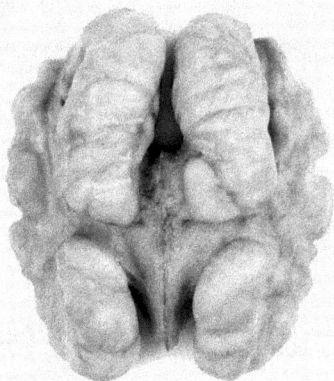

KETO BREAD ROLLS

NUTRITION (per serving)		
Total Carbs	8	grams
Fibre	6	grams
Net Carbs	2	grams
Protein	13	grams
Fat	7	grams
Calories	170	

Ingredients

- 125g/4oz almond flour
- 5 tbsp psyllium husk powder
- 2 tbsp sesame seeds
- 2 tsp baking powder
- 1 tsp of sea salt
- 250ml/8½floz boiling water
- 2 tsp of cider vinegar
- 3 egg whites

Method

1 Preheat the oven to 350F/180C/ Gas 4.

2 Place all the dry ingredients in a large bowl.

3 First, mix the vinegar and egg whites into the dry ingredients.

4 Now add the boiling water and beat the dough with a mixer for around one minute until you have a workable dough.

5 Use a little olive oil to prevent sticking while you shape the dough into 6 rolls.

6 Place the rolls on a baking sheet lightly greased with olive oil.

7 Sprinkle with sesame seeds.

8 Bake on the lower rack in the oven for 50–60 minutes. Test the rolls to see if they are done by tapping the bottom of the rolls. A hollow sound indicates the rolls are cooked through.

9 Serve warm or cold with butter.

CHEF'S NOTE
These high-fibre low-carb bread rolls are perfect served straight from the oven. You can also toast and freeze them with excellent results.

CREAMY BLACK PEPPER CABBAGE

NUTRITION (per serving)

Total Carbs	14	grams
Fibre	5	grams
Net Carbs	9	grams
Protein	5	grams
Fat	38	grams
Calories	401	

Ingredients

- 350g/12oz green cabbage, shredded
- 25g/1oz butter
- 150ml/5floz double cream
- 4 tbsp fresh parsley, finely chopped
- Salt and fresh black pepper

Method

1 Place the butter in a large heavy-based frying pan and melt over medium heat.

2 Sauté the cabbage for 3-5 minutes until soft and golden.

3 Stir in the double cream and leave to simmer for a few minutes further until the cream is reduced. Lower the heat to ensure the mixture doesn't stick.

4 Season to taste with freshly ground salt and black pepper.

5 Sprinkle over the chopped parsley.

CHEF'S NOTE

This indulgent and delicious side dish is perfect in place of mashed potatoes with meat and poultry dishes. It's thought cabbage may help reduce the levels of bad tau proteins that accumulate in Alzheimer's patients.

TURMERIC
CAULIFLOWER RICE

NUTRITION (per serving)

Total Carbs	10	grams
Fibre	4	grams
Net Carbs	6	grams
Protein	4	grams
Fat	19	grams
Calories	208	

Ingredients

- 350g/12oz cauliflower, grated
- 40g/1½oz butter
- ¼ tsp salt
- ¼ tsp turmeric

Method

1 Grate the cauliflower manually or with a food processor if you have a large quantity.

2 Melt the butter gently in a frying pan over medium heat.

3 Fry the cauliflower for 5-10 minutes, or until it has softened to your preference. Add the salt and turmeric during cooking.

4 Alternatively, you can microwave the cauliflower for 5-6 minutes in a covered bowl. Add the butter, salt, and turmeric after cooking.

CHEF'S NOTE
The chemical curcumin found in turmeric, has been shown to have antioxidant properties which could promote brain health and fight Alzheimer's. You could also change the seasoning to brain-boosting coriander, curry or garlic.

OVEN-BAKED CHILLI TURNIP WEDGES

NUTRITION (per serving)

Total Carbs	10	grams
Fibre	3	grams
Net Carbs	7	grams
Protein	1	grams
Fat	14	grams
Calories	167	

Ingredients

- 225g/8oz turnip
- ½ tsp chilli powder
- Salt and pepper
- 2 tbsp olive oil

Method

1 Preheat the oven to 400F/200C/ Gas 6.

2 Rinse and peel large or baby turnips. If using baby turnips, they will cook through quicker.

3 Cut the turnip into wedges and spread out to cover a baking tray.

4 Sprinkle with chilli powder, salt and pepper.

5 Drizzle olive oil over the wedges and toss to cover.

6 Bake in the oven for 20 minutes on the middle shelf.

7 The wedges are done with they are golden brown.

8 Use a spatula to remove the wedges carefully and serve immediately.

CHEF'S NOTE
These are a perfect low carb alternative to potato wedges. Turnips are high in vitamin C. It's thought that maintaining healthy vitamin C levels can have a protective effect against Alzheimer's.

COURGETTUCINNE

NUTRITION (per serving)

Total Carbs	10	grams
Fibre	3	grams
Net Carbs	7	grams
Protein	4	grams
Fat	29	grams
Calories	302	

Ingredients

- 2 courgettes, cut lengthways
- 50g/2oz butter
- Salt and pepper

Method

1 Deseed the courgette by using a spoon.

2 Use a mandolin or potato peeler to cut into thin strips.

3 Bring a large pan of salted water to the boil and add the courgette strips.

4 Cook for one minute then drain away the water.

5 Add the butter, salt and pepper.

6 Stir well and serve immediately.

CHEF'S NOTE

Courgette is high in various antioxidants thought to improve brain function. Serve as an alternative to fettucine with homemade meatballs, and pasta sauce. Or simply with fresh diced tomato, shaved parmesan and basil on top.

Total Carbs	7	grams
Fibre	3	grams
Net Carbs	4	grams
Protein	10	grams
Fat	28	grams
Calories	325	

SERVES 2

RADISH AND BACON STIR FRY

······················ *Ingredients* ·····················

- 140g/4½oz bacon, chopped
- 350g/12oz radishes, quartered
- 1 garlic clove, pressed
- Salt and pepper

······················ *Method* ·····················

1 Fry bacon in a large frying pan on medium-high heat for a few minutes.

2 Now add radishes and garlic and reduce to a medium heat.

3 Fry for about 10-15 minutes, stirring all the time.

4 The dish is cooked when the radishes have softened and have a good colour. Season with salt and pepper and serve immediately.

CHEF'S NOTE

This makes a delicious side dish in place of potatoes. You'll find that radishes lose their tartness as cooked. The high levels of vitamin C can help maintain brain function and slows memory decline.

CAULIFLOWER FRITTERS

SERVES 2

NUTRITION (per serving)

Total Carbs	9	grams
Fibre	3	grams
Net Carbs	6	grams
Protein	13	grams
Fat	15	grams
Calories	214	

Ingredients

- 350g/12oz cauliflower, rinsed and trimmed
- 1 tbsp olive oil
- 50g/2oz parmesan cheese, grated
- Salt and pepper

Method

1 Preheat the oven to 400F/200C/ Gas 6.

2 Slice the cauliflower in approximately 1cm thick slices from the head of the cauliflower to the base.

3 Line a baking tray with greaseproof paper and brush with olive oil.

4 Place the cauliflower slices on the tray and top with the cheese.

5 Bake in the oven for around 20-25 minutes or until brown.

CHEF'S NOTE
Cauliflower is high in vitamin C and antioxidants and can promote healthy brain function. Serve the fritters with chicken and meat dishes such as pork chops.

KETO ONION RINGS

NUTRITION (per serving)		
Total Carbs	6	grams
Fibre	1	grams
Net Carbs	5	grams
Protein	15	grams
Fat	26	grams
Calories	323	

Ingredients

- 1 large onion, peeled
- 1 egg
- 100g/3½oz almond flour
- 50g/2oz parmesan cheese, grated
- 1 tbsp olive oil
- 1 tsp garlic powder
- ½ tbsp chilli powder
- Salt and pepper

Method

1 Preheat the oven to 400F/200C/ Gas 6.

2 Slice the onion into rings, about ½ cm thick.

3 Mix the dry ingredients in a bag.

4 Whisk the egg in a bowl.

5 Dip the onion rings in the beaten egg and then shake in the flour bag, a few at a time.

6 Place the rings on a baking sheet lined with greaseproof paper.

7 Drizzle a little oil over the rings and bake for 15–20 minutes.

CHEF'S NOTE

Onions contain an antioxidant that binds with harmful toxins in the brain and flushes them out of the body. These healthy onion rings are delicious served with meat and steak.

CAULIFLOWER PUREE

NUTRITION (per serving)		
Total Carbs	8	grams
Fibre	4	grams
Net Carbs	4	grams
Protein	4	grams
Fat	3	grams
Calories	60	

Ingredients

- 1 medium head cauliflower, cut into florets
- 4 cloves garlic, crushed
- 75ml/2½floz reduced fat crème fraiche
- 1 tbsp reduced fat butter
- Salt and pepper to taste

Method

1 Steam the cauliflower with the garlic until soft.

2 Drain the cauliflower and place in a bowl.

3 Add the crème fraiche and butter and blend until smooth with a hand blender.

4 Season to taste with salt and pepper.

CHEF'S NOTE
This is a perfect keto alternative to mashed potatoes. It's also low in calories but you can add full fat butter and cream for a more luxurious version.

CHEESY CAULIFLOWER BAKE

NUTRITION (per serving)

Total Carbs	10	grams
Fibre	4	grams
Net Carbs	6	grams
Protein	2	grams
Fat	5	grams
Calories	112	

Ingredients

- 4 rashers bacon
- 675g/1½lb cauliflower florets
- 3 cloves garlic, crushed
- 1 tbsp reduced fat butter
- 75ml/2½floz reduced fat crème fraiche
- 2 tbsp fresh chives, finely chopped
- 50g/2oz reduced fat mature cheddar, grated
- Salt and black pepper, to taste

Method

1 Fry the bacon in a frying pan until crisp. Set aside on a paper towel.

2 Boil the cauliflower with the garlic for about 20 minutes until soft

3 Add the butter and crème fraiche and blend until smooth with a hand blender.

4 Stir in the chives and spoon into individual gratin dishes.

5 Scatter the cheese and crumbled bacon over the cauliflower.

6 Bake in the oven at 350F/180C/ Gas 4 for 5-10 minutes until the cheese has melted.

CHEF'S NOTE

This is delicious comfort food but low-calorie too! It's also rich in antioxidants and vitamin C for healthy brain function. You can add cream and more cheese if you're not watching your weight.

SERVES 4

ROASTED
SPAGHETTI SQUASH

NUTRITION (per serving)

Total Carbs	10	grams
Fibre	2	grams
Net Carbs	8	grams
Protein	1	grams
Fat	0	grams
Calories	42	

Ingredients

- 1 medium-sized ripe spaghetti squash
- Olive oil (optional)
- Salt and fresh pepper

Method

1 Preheat oven to 350F/180C/Gas 4.

2 Begin by cutting the squash in half and scooping out the seeds with a tablespoon.

3 Place the squash upside down and use a fork or skewer to pierce holes all the way through.

4 Place the squash on a baking tray cut side up. Drizzle with olive oil if using and season with salt and pepper.

5 Cook for approximately one hour. Use a fork to scrape at the squash and create spaghetti strands.

6 Serve immediately.

CHEF'S NOTE
Spaghetti squash is a perfect low-carb side dish. Try replacing any traditional pasta side with this spaghetti. Serve with meat, fish and classics such as Pomodoro or Bolognese Sauce.

SERVES 4

KETO POTATO SALAD

Total Carbs	13	grams
Fibre	8	grams
Net Carbs	7	grams
Protein	12	grams
Fat	30	grams
Calories	340	

Ingredients

- 60ml/2floz crème fraiche
- 120ml/4floz mayonnaise
- 2 tbsp white vinegar
- 1 tbsp mustard
- 1 tsp celery seeds
- ¼ tsp salt
- 900g/2lb cauliflower florets, steamed until tender and cooled.
- 4 large eggs, hard boiled and shelled
- 125g/4oz celery, diced
- 1 tsp fresh dill
- 2 spring onions, thinly sliced

Method

1 Place the mayonnaise, crème fraiche, vinegar, mustard, salt and celery seeds together in a small bowl and whisk until blended.

2 Chop the hardboiled eggs reserving two of the yolks.

3 Mash two of the egg yolks into the dressing and blend well.

4 Place the cauliflower, eggs, onions and celery into a large bowl and coat with the dressing.

5 Chill for one hour before serving.

CHEF'S NOTE

Cauliflower contains carotenoids and folate that helps retain memory by lowering levels of homocysteine, an amino acid linked with cognitive impairment.

BROCCOLI AND
CHEESE BAKE

NUTRITION (per serving)

Total Carbs	11	grams
Fibre	4	grams
Net Carbs	7	grams
Protein	11	grams
Fat	2	grams
Calories	172	

Ingredients

- 675g/1½lb broccoli florets
- 125g/4oz cheddar cheese, grated
- 1 tsp salt
- 1 tsp garlic powder

Method

1 Preheat oven to 350F/180C/ Gas 4.

2 Steam the broccoli until tender.

3 Place in an ovenproof baking dish so the broccoli is close together in a layer.

4 Sprinkle over the cheese, salt and garlic powder.

5 Bake for approximately 15 minutes or until the cheese is golden and bubbling.

6 Serve with meat or poultry.

CHEF'S NOTE
Broccoli is packed with vitamin C. Several bodies of evidence point to maintaining vitamin C levels being important in reducing the risk of Alzheimer's.

GARLIC BRUSSELS SPROUTS

NUTRITION (per serving)

Total Carbs	8	grams
Fibre	3	grams
Net Carbs	5	grams
Protein	4	grams
Fat	5	grams
Calories	81	

Ingredients

- 450g/1lb brussels sprouts, trimmed and halved
- 60ml/2floz olive oil
- 4 garlic cloves, crushed
- ½ tsp salt
- ¼ tsp pepper
- 150g/5oz goat's cheese, crumbled

Method

1 Preheat oven to 425F/225C/ Gas 7.

2 Toss all the ingredients except the cheese on a baking tray.

3 Roast for approximately 20-15 minutes or until tender.

4 Transfer to a bowl and mix in the cheese.

5 Serve immediately.

CHEF'S NOTE
Brussels sprouts are loaded with fat-soluble vitamin K that helps fight Alzheimer's. Serving the sprouts with the fat in the goat's cheese allows better absorption of nutrients.

LEEK DAUPHINOISE

NUTRITION (per serving)

Total Carbs	11	grams
Fibre	1	grams
Net Carbs	10	grams
Protein	5	grams
Fat	19	grams
Calories	224	

Ingredients

- 3 medium leeks, cut in half lengthwise and chopped into 5cm/2-inch pieces
- 175ml/6floz double cream
- 1 tsp sea salt
- ½ tsp pepper
- 50g/2oz pecorino Romano or parmesan, grated

Method

1 Preheat oven to 375F/190C/ Gas 5.

2 Place leeks, cream, salt and pepper in a large frying pan and bring to the boil.

3 Reduce the heat and simmer for around 15 minutes covered.

4 Simmer for a further 5 minutes uncovered.

5 Transfer the leeks to an ovenproof dish.

6 Top with the cheese.

7 Bake for 15-20 minutes until golden and bubbling.

CHEF'S NOTE
Leeks contain flavonoids which enhance detoxification by reducing toxins. This can help fight neurological illnesses including Alzheimer's.

SERVES 4

SLOW COOKED
HERBY MUSHROOMS

NUTRITION (per serving)

Total Carbs	4	grams
Fibre	2	grams
Net Carbs	2	grams
Protein	1	grams
Fat	2	grams
Calories	52	

Ingredients

- 450g/1lb whole fresh mushrooms
- 225g/8oz baby onions or shallots
- 4 garlic cloves, crushed
- 250ml/8½floz beef stock
- 60ml/2floz dry red wine
- 2 tbsp balsamic vinegar
- ½ tsp salt
- ½ tsp dried basil
- ½ tsp dried thyme
- ½ pepper
- ¼ crushed red pepper flakes

Method

1 Place mushrooms, onions and garlic in a large pan with a tight lid.

2 Add the stock, wine, vinegar, herbs and salt and pepper.

3 Bring to the boil and reduce to a simmer.

4 Cover the pan tightly and slowly cook for 2-3 hours. Check regularly to ensure the lid is secure and the mushrooms are not drying out or burning.

5 Alternatively, you can cook this dish in a slow cooker for around 6 hours.

6 Delicious served with steak, meat and poultry.

CHEF'S NOTE
Mushrooms contain a high amount of dietary fibre, and antioxidants as well as vitamins and minerals. It's thought that eating mushrooms can protect against cognitive decline and Alzheimer's.

71

SERVES 4

PARMESAN TOSSED CARROTS

Total Carbs	11	grams
Fibre	8	grams
Net Carbs	3	grams
Protein	2	grams
Fat	2	grams
Calories	72	

Ingredients

- 450g/1lb carrots, peeled
- 1 tsp olive oil
- ½ tsp salt
- ¼ tsp pepper
- ½ tsp dried thyme
- 3 tbsp parmesan cheese, grated

Method

1 Preheat oven to 450F/230C/ gas 8.

2 Cut carrots into 1cm/ ½-inch pieces.

3 Toss the carrots in the oil, thyme, salt and pepper.

4 Transfer the carrots to a baking tray.

5 Roast for approximately 15 minutes until tender.

6 Toss with the cheese before serving.

CHEF'S NOTE
Carrots contain ferulic acid which researchers believe may reverse Alzheimer's. They are also a good source of beta carotene, vitamin K1, and antioxidants thought to help fight Alzheimer's, too.

CHEESY PESTO BREAD TWISTS

NUTRITION (per serving)

Total Carbs	3	grams
Fibre	2	grams
Net Carbs	1	grams
Protein	7	grams
Fat	18	grams
Calories	204	

Ingredients

- 50g/2oz almond flour
- 25g/1oz coconut flour
- ½ tsp salt
- 1 tsp baking powder
- 300g/10½oz mozzarella, grated
- 75g/3oz butter
- 1 egg
- 50g/2oz green pesto
- 1 egg, beaten for glazing

Method

1 Preheat the oven to 350F/180C/Gas 4.

2 Mix all the dry ingredients together in a large bowl.

3 Melt the butter and cheese together in a heavy based saucepan over a low heat.

4 Stir the egg into the cheese mixture.

5 Add the dry ingredients and stir together to form a stiff dough.

6 Roll the dough in between 2 pieces of clingfilm to form a rectangle about ½ cm thick.

7 Spread the dough with pesto and then cut into 2cm/1-inch strips.

8 Twist the dough and place each on a baking tray.

9 Brush with beaten egg.

10 Bake for 15-20 minutes or until golden.

11 Serve as a snack or a side dish.

CHEF'S NOTE
The clever use of almond and coconut flour makes a bread twist with just 1 net gram of carbs!

TOMATOES PARMIGIANA

Ingredients

- 4 large tomatoes
- 40g/1½oz parmesan cheese, grated
- 1 tsp fresh oregano, chopped
- ¼ tsp salt
- 4 tsp extra-virgin olive oil
- Freshly ground pepper, to taste

Method

1 Preheat oven to 450F/230C/ gas 8.

2 Half the tomatoes horizontally.

3 Place the tomatoes with the cut side up on a baking tray.

4 Sprinkle with parmesan, oregano, salt and pepper.

5 Drizzle oil over the tomatoes.

6 Bake for 15 minutes or until the tomato is tender and the topping is golden.

7 Delicious served with meat and steaks.

CHEF'S NOTE
Tomatoes contain the flavanol fisetin which is thought to preserve brain health. They are also a great source of vitamin C, potassium, folate, and vitamin K.

Desserts

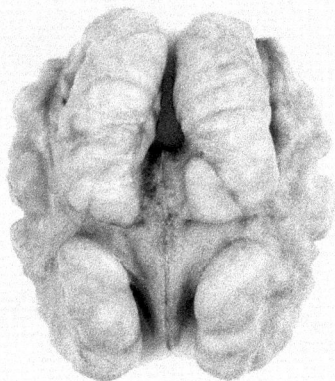

KETO
CHOCOLATE ROLL

NUTRITION (per serving)

Total Carbs	7	grams
Fibre	4	grams
Net Carbs	3	grams
Protein	5	grams
Fat	26	grams
Calories	269	

Ingredients

For the chocolate roll:
- 100g/3½oz almond flour
- 25g/1oz psyllium husk powder
- 50g/2oz cocoa powder
- 25g/1oz erythritol
- 1 tsp baking powder
- 3 large eggs
- 60ml/2floz melted butter
- 60ml/2floz sour milk
- 60ml/2floz coconut milk
- 1 tsp vanilla extract

For the cream cheese filling:
- 225g/8oz cream cheese
- 125g/4oz butter
- 60ml/2floz crème fraiche
- 75g/3oz erythritol
- 1 tsp of vanilla extract

Method

1 Preheat oven to 350F/180C/ Gas 4.

2 Combine the dry and wet ingredients in a large bowl and mix well.

3 Spread the dough onto a baking sheet and bake for 12- 15 minutes.

4 Combine the cream cheese ingredients in a small bowl.

5 Spread the filling over the cooled cake and roll together tightly.

CHEF'S NOTE
This super easy to make cake chocolate sponge roll gives you a perfect and indulgent chocolate hit. The flavonoids in cocoa are thought to improve mood and brain health.

CRUNCHY NUT KETO BERRY MOUSSE

NUTRITION (per serving)		
Total Carbs	5	grams
Fibre	2	grams
Net Carbs	3	grams
Protein	3	grams
Fat	27	grams
Calories	260	

Ingredients

- 250ml/8½floz double cream
- ¼ tsp vanilla extract
- ¼ lemon zest
- 25g/1oz pecans, chopped
- 40g/1½oz fresh berries e.g. raspberries, strawberries or blueberries

Method

1 Place the cream into a large bowl and whip until it is at the soft peaks stage.

2 Now add the vanilla extract and the lemon zest.

3 Fold in the chopped pecans and the fresh berries.

4 Cover with clingfilm and chill in the fridge until the mousse has set. This will take around three hours.

CHEF'S NOTE

Pecans are high in antioxidants and can help fight Alzheimer's. You can change the nuts, if you prefer and add berries such as cherries, red and blackcurrants.

CLASSIC KETO CHIA PUDDING

NUTRITION (per serving)

Total Carbs	15	grams
Fibre	8	grams
Net Carbs	7	grams
Protein	7	grams
Fat	44	grams
Calories	461	

Ingredients

- 175ml/6floz coconut milk
- 2 tbsp chia seeds
- ½ tsp vanilla extract

Method

1 Place all the ingredients together either in a bowl or a jar.

2 Simply mix or shake.

3 Place the pudding in the fridge to set. This needs to be at least 4 hours so that the seeds form a gel.

4 Serve the pudding with cream, coconut milk or some fresh or frozen berries.

5 It's also ideal as a breakfast dish.

CHEF'S NOTE
The omega 3 fatty acids in chia seeds are linked to a reduced risk of Alzheimer's. You can flavour the pudding with cinnamon, cocoa or peanut butter.

AVOCADO AND CHOC ICE LOLLIES

NUTRITION (per serving)

Total Carbs	3	grams
Fibre	1	grams
Net Carbs	2	grams
Protein	1	grams
Fat	4	grams
Calories	50	

Ingredients

- 2 medium avocados, halved
- 2 tbsp lemon juice
- 6 tbsp erythritol
- 250ml/8½floz unsweetened almond milk
- 75g/3oz 100% keto-friendly dark chocolate
- 15g/½oz cocoa butter

Method

1 Take out the stones from the avocados and scoop the flesh into a food processor.

2 Add the lemon juice, erythritol and almond milk and pulse until blended.

3 Spoon the mixture into ice lolly moulds and place in the freezer.

4 Melt the chocolate and cocoa butter gently in a bowl over a pan of boiling water.

5 When the melted chocolate has cooled dip the lollies in the chocolate.

6 Eat straightaway or return to the freezer.

CHEF'S NOTE
These low-calorie treats are delicious. You can buy sweetener and keto-friendly chocolate and cocoa butter online.

COCONUT
PANNA COTTA

NUTRITION (per serving)

Total Carbs	9	grams
Fibre	4	grams
Net Carbs	5	grams
Protein	7	grams
Fat	29	grams
Calories	319	

Ingredients

- 175g/6oz coconut cream
- 100g/3½oz, almonds blanched
- 60g/2½oz erythritol
- 175ml/6floz unsweetened almond milk
- 75ml/2½floz unsweetened coconut milk
- 1 tsp powdered gelatine
- 2 tbsp coconut water
- ½ tsp orange oil

Method

1 Place the coconut cream in the fridge for it to chill and become thick.

2 Place the almonds in a food processor and blitz to create an almond butter.

3 Mix the almonds, sweetener, almond milk and coconut milk in a small non-stick saucepan.

4 Bring to the boil gently, stirring all the time until the erythritol has dissolved.

5 Dissolve the gelatine in the coconut water.

6 When dissolved add to the milk mixture and whisk in the orange oil.

7 Once the mixture has cooled and become thicker, fold in the chilled coconut cream.

8 Spoon the mixture into 4 individual ramekins and chill in the fridge to completely set.

CHEF'S NOTE
Almonds have more alpha-tocopherol vitamin E than almost any other food. Eating a diet high in vitamin E is associated with a reduced risk of Alzheimer's.

RASPBERRY VODKA FROZEN YOGHURT

NUTRITION (per serving)

Total Carbs	6	grams
Fibre	2	grams
Net Carbs	4	grams
Protein	8	grams
Fat	7	grams
Calories	114	

Ingredients

For the frozen yoghurt:
- 250ml/8½floz Greek full-fat yoghurt
- 125g/4oz raspberries frozen
- 1 tbsp coconut oil
- 1 tbsp vanilla whey powder
- Erythritol drops, to taste
- 1 dash salt
- 2 tbsp vodka

For the sesame topping:
- 1 tbsp sesame seeds
- 2 tbsp syrup sweetener
- 1 tsp cinnamon

Method

1 Put all the ingredients for the frozen yoghurt into a food processor.

2 Pulse the mixture until it's all incorporated. Scrape down the sides with a spatula.

3 Pour into an airtight container and place in the freezer.

4 Place the sesame seeds in the microwave and heat on high for a few seconds until you can begin to smell them roasting.

5 Stir in the cinnamon and sweetener and pour over the frozen yoghurt.

CHEF'S NOTE
Adding the vodka to this recipe allows you to freeze the yoghurt without getting large ice crystals.

KETO LEMON BARS

NUTRITION (per serving)

Total Carbs	9	grams
Fibre	4	grams
Net Carbs	5	grams
Protein	7	grams
Fat	29	grams
Calories	272	

Ingredients

- 125g/4oz butter, melted
- 175g/6oz almond flour
- 200g/7oz erythritol
- 3 medium lemons
- 3 large eggs

Method

1 Preheat the oven to 350F/180C/ Gas 4.

2 Line an 8-inch/20-cm square tin with greaseproof paper.

3 Mix the melted butter with 100g/3½oz almond flour and 50g/2oz erythritol.

4 Press the mixture into the tin.

5 Bake for 20 minutes. Leave to cool.

6 Place the zest from 1 lemon and the juice from 3 lemons into a bowl. Add the remaining almond flour and erythritol and whisk to combine.

7 Pour the lemon filling over the base and return to the oven for 20-30 minutes.

8 Leave to cool before cutting into 8 slices.

CHEF'S NOTE
It's thought that flavonoid-rich lemon juice could help in the Alzheimer's fight. Relax and enjoy with a cup of brain boosting coffee.

KETO KONJAC RICE PUDDING

NUTRITION (per serving)

Total Carbs	7	grams
Fibre	2	grams
Net Carbs	5	grams
Protein	4	grams
Fat	45	grams
Calories	460	

Ingredients

- 250g/9oz konjac rice
- 500ml/1¼pts double cream
- 1 vanilla pod
- 1 stick cinnamon
- 1 star anise
- 3 cardamom seeds
- 1 tbsp butter
- 75g/3oz dried cherries

Method

1 First prepare the rice. Wash the rice in a sieve and place in a pan of boiling water.

2 Cook for 3 minutes and strain.

3 Return the rice to the saucepan with the vanilla, cinnamon, star anise, cardamom with 1 pint of the cream.

4 Cook over a low heat for 15-20 minutes.

5 Remove from the heat and cool for a few minutes.

6 Carefully remove the vanilla pod, cinnamon stick and star anise before stirring in the butter, remaining cream and cherries.

CHEF'S NOTE

Konjac rice is sometimes referred to as ketogenic rice. It's made up of fibre from the root of the konjac plant. It's also great for slimmers with just 10 calories per 100 grams.

MAKES 8

KETO VANILLA BEAN CUPCAKES

NUTRITION (per serving)

Total Carbs	6	grams
Fibre	2	grams
Net Carbs	4	grams
Protein	7	grams
Fat	30	grams
Calories	329	

Ingredients

For the cupcakes:
- 2 large eggs
- 120ml/4floz mayonnaise
- 1 tsp vanilla extract
- 200g/7oz cups almond flour
- 125g/4oz erythritol
- ¼ tsp salt
- 2 tsp baking powder

For the frosting:
- 125g/4oz cream cheese
- 50g/2oz powdered erythritol
- 3 tbsp double cream
- ½ tsp vanilla extract

Method

1 Preheat oven to 350F/180C/Gas4.

2 Place the eggs, mayonnaise and vanilla extract in a bowl and whisk with an electric whisk until well blended.

3 Add the dry ingredients and mix in again, slowly to begin with.

4 The mixture will be quite stiff. Divide into 8 muffin tins using a tablespoon.

5 Bake for 20-25 minutes. The cakes are done when they are golden brown.

6 To make the frosting place the ingredients in a small bowl and mix together.

7 Pipe or spoon the frosting onto the cooled cakes and enjoy.

CHEF'S NOTE
Erythritol is a great keto and healthy ingredient. It's a sugar alcohol which has virtually zero calories. You can use it in place of table sugar in the ratio of 1 cup sugar to 1 1/3 cups erythritol.

QUICK CHOCOLATE KETO MUG CAKE

NUTRITION (per serving)

Total Carbs	8	grams
Fibre	3	grams
Net Carbs	5	grams
Protein	7	grams
Fat	19	grams
Calories	219	

Ingredients

- 1 tbsp coconut flour
- 1 tbsp unsweetened cocoa powder
- 1 tbsp erythritol
- ¼ tsp baking powder

- 1 large egg
- 1 tbsp melted butter
- 1 tbsp unsweetened almond milk

Method

1 Combine the dry ingredients in a bowl.

2 Pour on the wet ingredients and mix thoroughly.

3 Pour into a mug greased with butter.

4 Cook in the microwave on high for 2 minutes.

5 Serve with whipped cream.

CHEF'S NOTE

If you're in need of a quick chocolate fix, this is it! Cocoa has been hailed as a superfood for its antioxidant and flavonoid content thought to help the fight against Alzheimer's.

KETO BROWNIES

NUTRITION (per serving)		
Total Carbs	10	grams
Fibre	4	grams
Net Carbs	6	grams
Protein	4	grams
Fat	16	grams
Calories	172	

Ingredients

- 150g/5oz low-carb dark chocolate
- 50g/2oz butter
- 3 large eggs
- 115g/4oz erythritol
- 50g/2oz mascarpone cheese
- 25g/1oz cocoa powder
- ½ tsp salt

Method

1 Heat oven to 375F/190C/Gas 5.

2 Grease and line an 20cm/8-inch square baking tin with greaseproof paper.

3 Melt the chocolate in the microwave carefully on medium heat.

4 Add the butter and continue heating in the microwave at short intervals of 10 seconds.

5 Beat eggs and erythritol together with an electric hand whisk until frothy and pale.

6 Beat in the mascarpone cheese until smooth.

7 Fold in the sifted cocoa and salt gradually a tablespoon at a time until incorporated.

8 Then fold in the chocolate butter mixture.

9 Pour into the tin and bake for around 25 minutes.

KETO GINGERSNAP COOKIES

NUTRITION (per serving)

Total Carbs	2	grams
Fibre	1	grams
Net Carbs	1	grams
Protein	2	grams
Fat	7	grams
Calories	78	

Ingredients

- 250g/9oz almond flour
- 5g/2oz unsalted butter, melted
- 225g/8oz erythritol
- 1 large egg, beaten
- 1 tsp vanilla extract
- ¼ tsp salt
- 2 tsp ginger
- ¼ tsp nutmeg
- ¼ tsp cloves
- ½ tsp cinnamon

Method

1 Preheat oven to 350F/180C/ Gas 4.

2 Mix the dry ingredient together in a large bowl.

3 Pour in the wet ingredients and mix well.

4 Use a tablespoon to drop cookies onto two lined baking trays.

5 Flatten each cookie down a little.

6 Bake for 10-12 minutes or lightly brown.

7 Leave to cool before storing in an airtight container.

CHEF'S NOTE

Ginger contains the naturally occurring antioxidant curcumin. This anti-inflammatory property is important since many brain disorders including depression, brain fog and Alzheimer's are linked to chronic inflammation of the brain.

KETO RASPBERRY PAVLOVAS

NUTRITION (per serving)

Total Carbs	8	grams
Fibre	3	grams
Net Carbs	5	grams
Protein	5	grams
Fat	21	grams
Calories	290	

Ingredients

For the meringue:
- 4 large egg whites
- 50g/2oz erythritol
- 1 tsp lemon juice
- 2 tsp xanthan gum

For the filling
- 250ml/8½floz double cream, whipped
- 165g/5½oz raspberries

Method

1 Preheat oven to 300F/130C/ Gas 2.

2 Line two baking sheets with grease proof paper and draw around a saucer or small plates to mark out 4 pavlovas.

3 Beat egg whites until foamy with an electric whisk.

4 Add the erythritol gradually and continue to beat until all the erythritol has been added and the mixture forms stiff peaks.

5 Fold in the lemon juice and xanthan gum with a spatula.

6 Spoon the mixture onto the baking trays using the back of a spoon to shape the pavlovas.

7 Bake for an hour until dry and golden brown.

8 To prepare the filling, reserve 20 of the best raspberries for decoration.

9 Fold the remaining raspberries into the cream.

10 Spoon the filling into the pavlovas and top with individual raspberries.

KETO AMARETTI COOKIES

NUTRITION (per serving)

Total Carbs	2	grams
Fibre	1	grams
Net Carbs	1	grams
Protein	2	grams
Fat	8	grams
Calories	89	

Ingredients

- 100g/3½oz almond flour
- 15g/½oz coconut flour
- ½ tsp baking Powder
- ¼ tsp cinnamon
- ½ tsp salt
- 125g/4oz erythritol
- 2 eggs
- 60ml/2floz coconut oil, melted
- ½ tsp vanilla extract
- ½ tsp almond extract
- 2 tbsp sugar-free raspberry or cherry jam
- 1 tbsp desiccated coconut

Method

1 Preheat oven to 350F/180C/ Gas 4.

2 Line a baking tray with greaseproof paper.

3 Combine all dry ingredients.

4 Add wet ingredients and mix well.

5 Drop the cookies onto baking tray.

6 Add an indent in the middle of each cookie using your finger.

7 Bake for about 16 minutes or until the cookies turn golden.

8 Let the cookies cool on a wire rack and spoon a little jam into the well.

9 Sprinkle some shredded coconut on top of each one and enjoy!

CHEF'S NOTE

Almonds are made of a protein which helps repair brain cells and improve memory. They are rich in vitamin E and zinc which reduce free radicals and slow down the ageing process of brain cells.

KETO APPLE COBBLER

NUTRITION (per serving)

Total Carbs	10	grams
Fibre	3	grams
Net Carbs	7	grams
Protein	7	grams
Fat	19	grams
Calories	226	

Ingredients

For the filling:
- 4 chayote squash, peeled and sliced
- 25g/1oz butter, cut into small pieces to dot the filling
- 60ml/2floz lemon juice
- ½ tsp cream of tartar
- 75g/3oz erythritol

For the cobbler topping:
- 2 large eggs
- 150g/5oz almond flour
- 50g/2oz coconut flour
- 50g/2oz butter (sliced into small pieces)
- 1 tsp baking powder
- 25g/1oz erythritol

Method

1 Pre-heat the oven to 350C/180F/ Gas 4.

2 Boil the whole chayote with enough water to cover them for 30 minutes.

3 Place the chayote into a bowl and leave to cool.

4 Add the erythritol, cream of tartar and lemon juice, stir well and place in a greased 22cm/9inch pie dish.

5 To make the cobbler place the dry ingredients into a large bowl.

6 Rub the butter into the dry ingredients until it resembles breadcrumbs.

7 Stir in the egg then scatter the crumb mixture over the chayote.

8 Dot the filling with butter.

9 Bake for around 35 minutes until golden and bubbling.

10 Serve with whipped cream or custard.

CHEF'S NOTE
Chayote squash taste a little like apple crossed with potato and pear. The squash helps to keep the net carbs to just 7 grams per portion. They're also high in Alzheimer's-fighting folates and vitamin C.

KETO DEATH BY CHOCOLATE CAKE

NUTRITION (per serving)

Total Carbs	22	grams
Fibre	3	grams
Net Carbs	19	grams
Protein	6	grams
Fat	2	grams
Calories	252	

Ingredients

For the cake:
- 200g/7oz almond flour
- 100g/3 ½ oz erythritol
- 50g/2oz cocoa powder
- 1 tsp baking powder
- 100g/4oz butter, softened
- 1 tsp vanilla extract
- 2 eggs
- 250ml/8½floz unsweetened almond milk

For the frosting:
- 225g/8oz cream cheese, softened
- 125g/4oz butter, softened
- 50g/2oz powdered erythritol
- 1 tsp vanilla extract
- 3 tbsp cocoa powder
- 2 tbsp double cream

Method

1 Preheat the oven to 350F/180C/ Gas 4.

2 In a large bowl, mix the dry ingredients together.

3 Add the butter and eggs and mix using an electric whisk on high until the mixture is well blended and smooth.

4 Pour the cake mixture evenly into the three 15cm/6-inch sandwich tins and bake for 20-25 minutes or until the cake is cooked through in the middle. You can test by making sure a skewer comes out clean.

5 Make the frosting by whisking all the ingredients together with an electric hand whisk for a few minutes until fluffy.

6 To assemble place one third of the frosting on the first cake and smooth over the top and sides.

7 Put the second layer on the first and repeat the process with remaining layers.

CHEF'S NOTE
Cocoa is rich in flavonoids which boost blood flow to the brain.

KETO BAKED EGG CUSTARD TART

NUTRITION (per serving)		
Total Carbs	8	grams
Fibre	4	grams
Net Carbs	4	grams
Protein	4	grams
Fat	18	grams
Calories	212	

Ingredients

For the pastry:
- 120ml/4floz coconut oil
- 2 eggs
- 1 tbsp erythritol
- ¼ tsp salt
- 100g/3½ oz coconut flour

For the custard:
- 300ml/10½floz unsweetened almond milk
- 2 tsp vanilla extract
- 3 eggs
- 50g/2oz erythritol
- 1 tsp nutmeg

Method

1 Pre-heat oven to 400F/200C/ Gas 6.

2 Place all the pastry ingredients together in a medium bowl and beat together to form a dough.

3 Pat the dough into a 20cm/8-inch greased tart pan.

4 Prick the dough with a fork and blind bake for 8-10 minutes.

5 Reduce oven to 300F/150/Gas 2.

6 Heat the almond milk and vanilla in a small heavy based pan until just before boiling.

7 Beat the eggs and erythritol in a medium bowl.

8 Add the milk slowly so the eggs are not cooked.

9 Pour the custard into the tart base standing on a baking tray.

10 Sprinkle with nutmeg and bake for 30-40 minutes until the custard has set.

11 Serve warm or cold in slices.

SERVES 4

LEMON SOUFFLES

NUTRITION (per serving)

Total Carbs	3	grams
Fibre	0	grams
Net Carbs	3	grams
Protein	10	grams
Fat	11	grams
Calories	155	

Ingredients

- 2 large eggs, separated
- 250g/9oz ricotta
- 2 tsp lemon zest
- 1 tbsp lemon juice
- 50g/2oz erythritol

Method

1 Preheat your oven to 375F/190C/ Gas 5.

2 Grease 4 ramekins.

3 Beat the egg whites until foamy.

4 Add in 2 tbsp of erythritol and whisk until shiny and stiff like meringue.

5 Beat the ricotta, egg yolks, lemon juice and zest and remaining erythritol.

6 Fold the egg whites into the egg yolks gently to keep the air.

7 Pour the souffle batter into the ramekin.

8 Bake for approximately 20 minutes until just set.

9 Serve immediately.

CHEF'S NOTE
The use of erythritol keeps the net carbs to just 3 grams and the calories just 155 per portion.

STRAWBERRY PUFF CAKES

Total Carbs	6	grams
Fibre	1	grams
Net Carbs	5	grams
Protein	8	grams
Fat	33	grams
Calories	341	

Ingredients

For the puffs:
- 3 large eggs, separated
- 75g/3oz cream cheese
- ¼ tsp baking powder
- ½ tsp vanilla extract
- 2 tbsp erythritol

For the filling:
- 125g/4oz strawberries, chopped
- 250ml/8½floz double cream, whipped
- Erythritol to taste

Method

1 Preheat oven to 300F/150C/ Gas 2.

2 Beat the egg whites until they form soft peaks.

3 In a large bowl mix together the cream cheese, egg yolks, baking powder, vanilla and erythritol until smooth.

4 Fold the egg whites into the mixture with a large spoon.

5 Spread the mixture onto a lined baking sheet with a spatula to make 8 disks.

6 Bake for approximately 25 minutes or until puffed up and golden.

7 Leave to cool.

8 Mix the strawberries with the whipped cream.

9 Sweeten if desired.

10 Sandwich 2 puffs together with the cream mixture.

CHEF'S NOTE
A natural flavanol found in strawberries called fisetin could help to prevent Alzheimer's disease and other age-related neurodegenerative diseases.

MINI KEY LIME CHEESECAKES

NUTRITION (per serving)

Total Carbs	3	grams
Fibre	1	grams
Net Carbs	2	grams
Protein	4	grams
Fat	22	grams
Calories	217	

Ingredients

For the cheesecake crust:
- 50g/2oz macadamia or brazil nuts, ground until coarse
- 50g/2oz erythritol
- 50g/2oz almond flour
- 1 large egg yolk
- 50g/2oz butter, chilled

For the filling:
- 225g/8oz cream cheese
- 50g/2oz butter
- 2 large eggs
- 2 tbsp lime juice
- Zest of 2 limes
- 50g/2oz erythritol
- ¼ tsp liquid sweetener

Method

1 Preheat oven to 350F/180C/ Gas 4.

2 Place the nuts, erythritol and almond flour in a food processor and pulse for 1 minute.

3 Add the egg yolk and butter and pulse until a sticky dough is formed.

4 Mould the dough into 12 muffin tins.

5 Bake for 5-7minutes. Leave to cool.

6 Make the filling by creaming together the cream cheese, butter, eggs, lime juice, zest and sweetener until fluffy.

7 Pour the filling mix into the crust cases.

8 Bake again for approximately 30 minutes or until set.

9 Leave to cool then refrigerate.

CHEF'S NOTE
Macadamia and brazil nuts are a good source of selenium. A deficiency in selenium has been linked to Alzheimer's so try to maintain your levels.

CINNAMON CAKE

NUTRITION (per serving)

Total Carbs	7	grams
Fibre	3	grams
Net Carbs	4	grams
Protein	13	grams
Fat	28	grams
Calories	320	

Ingredients

For the base:
- 6 eggs, separated
- ¼ tsp cream of tartar
- 175g/6oz cream cheese
- 50g/2oz erythritol
- ¼ tsp liquid stevia
- 25g/1oz protein powder
- 2 tsp vanilla extract

For the filling:
- 150g/5oz almond flour
- 1 tbsp cinnamon
- 50g/2oz butter
- 60ml/2floz liquid sweetener
- 50g/2oz erythritol

Method

1 Preheat oven to 325F/160C/ Gas3.

2 Whisk the egg whites with the cream of tartar until it forms stiff peaks.

3 Cream erythritol, egg yolks, cream cheese, stevia, protein powder, and vanilla extract together.

4 Fold the egg whites gently into the mixture to keep the cake light and airy.

5 Make the filling by mixing all ingredients together to form a stiff dough.

6 Pour base mixture into a greased and lined 18cm/7-inch deep cake tin.

7 Now drop the dough filling into the batter. Bake for 40-50 minutes.

8 Test the cake with a skewer to make sure it is cooked through.

9 Serve with whipped cream and good coffee.

CHEF'S NOTE
Almond flour is a good source in vitamin E that acts as an antioxidant in your body. Higher vitamin E intakes have been linked to lower rates of Alzheimer's.